Chapter 1: Breakfast Smoothies

   The Breakfast Margarita

   Homely Honeydew Twist

   The Sweet Melon Morning Kale

   The Ultimate Morning Green

   Fine Liquid Sunrise

   Morning Aloha Smoothie

   The Banana Delight

   The Raspberry Minty Delight

   The Rising Red Sun

   Cinnamon And Beet Booster Dose

Chapter 2: Smoothies That Nourish Your Brain

   The Wisest Watermelon Glass

   Cheery Charlie Checker

   The Pom Drink

   Bright Rainbow Health

   Great Nutty Lion

   A Whole Melon Surprise

   Muscular Macho Green

   Buddha's Banana Berry

   Brain Nutrition-Analyzer

   Complete Banana Meal

Chapter 3: Alkalizing Smoothies Protect Your Boned And Kidneys

   Smoothie Vegetable Blast

   Strawberry Banana Yogurt Smoothie

   Cantaloupe Lettuce Smoothie

Powerful Alkaline Smoothie
  Alkaline Breakfast Breaker
  Mixed Berry Smoothie
  Sweet Kale Smoothie
  Almond Butter Berry Smoothie
  Green Smoothie Bowl
  The Flat Belly Smoothie

Chapter 4: Anti-Aging Smoothies
  Mango And Blueberry Bean Smoothie
  Pineapple Green Anti-Ager
  Apple Cherry Pumpkin Tea
  Beets And Berry Beauty Enhancer
  A Honeydew And Cucumber Medley
  Natural Nectarine
  Fine Tea Toner
  The Grapefruit Glow
  The Anti-Aging Avocado
  A Green Grape Shake

Chapter 5: Anti-Oxidant Smoothies
  Berry-Licious Anti-Oxidant Banana Smoothie
  Protein-Packed Anti-Oxidizer
  Triple Berry Supreme
  A Green Grape Shake
  The Flaxseed Anti-Oxidizer
  Mixed Berry And Kiwi Medley
  Supreme Green Tea Glass

Pomegranate Anti-Oxidizer

Anti-Oxi Boosting Rolled Oats Smoothie

Anti-Oxi Rich Almond Flavored Smoothie

Chapter 6: Cleansing Smoothies

A Melon Cucumber Medley

Kale And Beet 2021 Fusion

Strawberry And Watermelon Medley

Punchy Watermelon

Hearty Cucumber Quencher

Dandelion Aloha

Blueberry Detox Drink

Cocoa Pumpkin

Twisty Cucumber Honeydew

Chocolaty Pleasure Delight

Chapter 7: Diabetic Smoothies

Berry-Licious Meta Booster

Healthy Potato Pie Glass

Vegetable And Green Tea Smoothie

Tropical Kiwi Pineapple

Greens And Herbs For All

Avocado And Edamame Drink

Peanut Butter And Cherry Delight

White Bean And Mango Delight

Cashew Apple Glass

Spicy Pear And Green Tea

Chapter 8: Digestive Health Smoothies

Tropical Storm Glass

Cool Strawberry 365

Noteworthy Vitamin C

Hearty Papaya Drink

A Minty Drink

The Baked Apple

The Amazing Acai

Fine Yo "Mama" Matcha

The Pumpkin Eye

Great Green Garden

Chapter 9: High-Energy Smoothies

Generous Mango Surprise

Powerful Purple Smoothie

Banana Apple Blast

Energizing Pineapple Kicker

Dandelion And Carrot Booster

Green Skinny Energizer

Awesome Pineapple And Carrot Blend

Mango Energizer

Powerful Green Frenzy

Chapter 10: Green Smoothies Recipes

The Minty Cucumber

Lemon Cilantro Delight

A Peachy Medley

Cilantro And Citrus Glass

The Deep Green Lagoon

The Wild Matcha Delight

The Green Potato Chai

Lemon Cilantro Delight

Lovely Green Gazpacho

Tropical Matcha Kale

Chapter 11: Healthful Skin Recipes

Evergreen Morning Dew

Awesome Baby-Face Maker

Exotic Reishi Pear

The Savior Of Skin

Tangy Citrus Glass

Hearty Sweet Basil

The Purifier

Kiwi Cucumber Delight

The Funky Skin Refresher

The Glamorous Radiance

Chapter 12: Kid-Friendly Smoothies

Delicious Creamy Choco Shake

Mesmerizing Strawberry And Chocolate Shake

The Overloaded Berry Shake

The Blueberry And Chocolate Delight

Cool Coco-Loco Cream Shake

Healthy Chocolate Milkshake

The Cacao Super Smoothie

The Nutty Smoothie

The Strawberry Almond Smoothie

Mixed Fruit Madness

Chapter 13: Low-Fat Smoothies

The Big Blue Delight

The Big Bomb Pop

The Pinky Swear

A Peachy Perfect Glass

Slim-Jim Vanilla Latte

Cauliflower Cold Glass

A Batch Of Slimming Berries

Fine Green Machine

The Summer Hearty Shake

The Mocha Built

Chapter 14: Protein Smoothies

Sweet Protein And Cherry Shake

Iron And Protein Shake

Creamy Peachy Shake

Protein-Packed Root Beer Shake

Almond And Choco-Brownie Shake

Raspberry And White Chocolate Shake

Peppermint And Dark Chocolate Shake Delight

Spiced Up Banana Shake

Mad Mocha Glass

Lemon And Cranberry Shake

Chapter 15: Weight-Loss Smoothies

Hearty Dandelion Smoothie

Apple And Zucchini Medley

Flax And Kiwi Spinach Smoothie
Cucumber Kale And Lime Apple Smoothie
Banana And Spinach Raspberry Smoothie
Flax And Almond Butter Smoothie
Leeks And Broccoli Cucumber Glass
Straight Up Avocado And Kale Smoothie
Apple Broccoli Smoothie
Zucchini Apple Smoothie

Chapter 16: Alkaline Smoothies
Strawberry And Clementine Mix
Strawberry And Watermelon Smoothie
Watermelon Berry Smoothie
Cucumber And Spinach Glass
Broccoli Green Smoothie
A Sweet Green Mix
Almond And Spinach Glass
Pear And Kale Glass
Peach And Banana Glass
Almond And Carrot Smoothie
Protein Spinach Shake
Basil Strawberry Delight
Cabbage And Chia Delight
Grapefruit Spinach Smoothie
Plain Coconut Smoothie
Lovely Detox Smoothie
Blueberry Avocado Smoothie

Lemon And Pineapple Smoothie
Raspberry Chia Seeds
Avocado And Orange Glass
Apricot And Spinach Smoothie
Cantaloupe Lemon Smoothie
Frosty Watermelon Smoothie
Lush Cherry Mix
Crafty Cucumber Smoothie
Balanced Alkaline Veggie Cubes
Blueberry And Banana Smoothie
Pineapple Green Smoothie
Tri-Berry Smoothie
Alkaline Lime Smoothie
The Antioxidant Booster
Raw Green Smoothie
The Green Goddess
Morning Alkaline Blend
Original Sleepy Bug
Coconut And Mango Meal
Tangy Lettuce Detox
Tri-Berry Banana Smoothie
Nut Packed Papaya Meal
Dandelion Greens
Cucumber And Tamarind Meal
Clean Cantaloupe Smoothie
Refreshing Watermelon Breather

Watercress Detox Delight

Figs Smoothie

Hearty Green Glass

Classic Banana And Ginger Mix

The Ginger And Kale Ale

Anti-Oxidizing Glass

Fresh Orange Smoothie

Tart Cherry and Greens Smoothie

Beans, Peaches and Greens Smoothie

Chapter 1: Breakfast Smoothies
1. The Breakfast Margarita

Serving: 2

Prep Time: 5 minutes

Ingredients

- 1 tablespoon hemp seeds
- ½ a lime, juiced
- ¼ fresh avocado
- 2 mandarin oranges
- 1 cup of frozen strawberries
- 1 cup unsweetened coconut milk

Directions

1. Add all the ingredients except vegetables/fruits first
2. Blend until smooth
3. Add the vegetable/fruits
4. Blend until smooth
5. Add a few ice cubes and serve the smoothie

Nutrition Values

- Calories: 234
- Fat: 8g
- Carbohydrates: 40g
- Protein: 6g

2. Homely Honeydew Twist

Serving: 2

Prep Time: 5 minutes

Ingredients

- 1 cup ice
- 1 tablespoon fresh mint
- 2 cucumbers, chopped
- 1 cup honeydew melon, peeled and seeded, chopped
- 1 cup of coconut water

Directions

1. Add all the ingredients except vegetables/fruits first
2. Blend until smooth
3. Add the vegetable/fruits
4. Blend until smooth
5. Add a few ice cubes and serve the smoothie
6. Enjoy!

Nutrition Values

- Calories: 190
- Fat: 2g
- Carbohydrates: 35g
- Protein: 2g

3. The Sweet Melon Morning Kale

Serving: 2

Prep Time: 5 minutes

Ingredients

- 1 tablespoon lemon juice
- 1 medium cucumber, diced
- 1 cup honeydew melon, peeled and chopped
- 4 cups kale, chopped

Directions

1. Add all the ingredients except vegetables/fruits first
2. Blend until smooth
3. Add the vegetable/fruits
4. Blend until smooth
5. Add a few ice cubes and serve the smoothie

Nutrition Values
- Calories: 143
- Fat: 2g
- Carbohydrates: 30g
- Protein: 2g

4. The Ultimate Morning Green

Serving: 2

Prep Time: 5 minutes

Ingredients

- 1 medium whole tomato, diced
- 2 cups baby spinach, chopped
- 1 medium sweet green pepper, chopped
- 15 green grapes
- 1 cucumber, cubed
- 2 medium carrots, scrubbed and chopped
- 2 medium Granny Smith apples, quartered

Directions

1. Add all the ingredients except vegetables/fruits first
2. Blend until smooth
3. Add the vegetable/fruits
4. Blend until smooth
5. Add a few ice cubes and serve the smoothie

Nutrition Values

- Calories: 203
- Fat: 1g
- Carbohydrates: 51g
- Protein: 4g

5. Fine Liquid Sunrise

Serving: 2

Prep Time: 5 minutes

Ingredients

- 1 cup ice
- 4 tablespoons protein powder
- 1 cup of frozen mango, sliced
- 1 cup of frozen strawberries
- 1 cup baby spinach
- 1 and ¾ cup unsweetened coconut milk drink

Directions

1. Add all the ingredients except vegetables/fruits first
2. Blend until smooth
3. Add the vegetable/fruits
4. Blend until smooth
5. Add a few ice cubes and serve the smoothie

Nutrition Values
- Calories: 196
- Fat: 2g
- Carbohydrates: 22g
- Protein: 13g

6. Morning Aloha Smoothie

Serving: 2

Prep Time: 5 minutes

Ingredients

- 1 cup ice
- 1 tablespoon coconut, shredded
- 1 cup of frozen mango, sliced
- ¾ cup pineapple sliced
- 1 and ½ cups unsweetened almond milk

Directions

1. Add all the ingredients except vegetables/fruits first
2. Blend until smooth
3. Add the vegetable/fruits
4. Blend until smooth
5. Add a few ice cubes and serve the smoothie

Nutrition Values

- Calories: 121g
- Fat: 6g
- Carbohydrates: 18g
- Protein: 1g

7. The Banana Delight

Serving: 2

Prep Time: 5 minutes

Ingredients

- 1 cup ice
- 2 tablespoons protein powder
- 1 tablespoon green superfood as preferred
- 1 frozen banana, cubed
- 1 cup baby spinach
- 1 cup unsweetened almond milk

Directions

1. Add all the ingredients except vegetables/fruits first
2. Blend until smooth
3. Add the vegetable/fruits
4. Blend until smooth
5. Add a few ice cubes and serve the smoothie

Nutrition Values

- Calories: 150
- Fat: 4g
- Carbohydrates: 26g
- Protein: 4g

8. The Raspberry Minty Delight

Serving: 2

Prep Time: 5 minutes

Ingredients

- 1 cup ice
- 1 teaspoon probiotics
- 1 tablespoon fresh mint
- ½ frozen banana, sliced
- 2 cups frozen raspberries
- 1 and ½ cups unsweetened almond milk

Directions

1. Add all the ingredients except vegetables/fruits first
2. Blend until smooth
3. Add the vegetable/fruits
4. Blend until smooth
5. Add a few ice cubes and serve the smoothie

Nutrition Values

- Calories: 75
- Fat: 2g
- Carbohydrates: 13g
- Protein: 2g

9. The Rising Red Sun

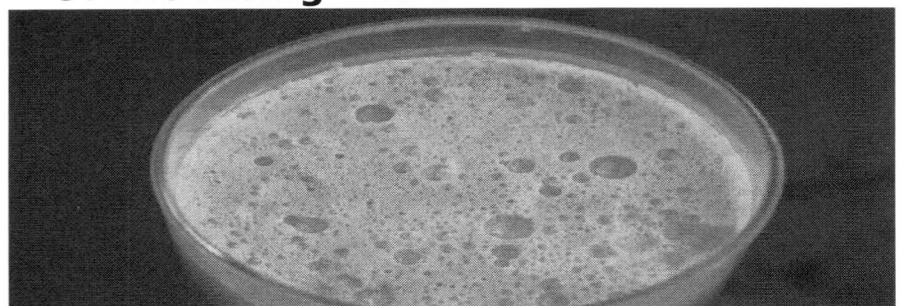

Serving: 2

Prep Time: 5 minutes

Ingredients

- ¼ lemon, sliced
- ¼ Barlett pear, cored
- 1 medium beet, scrubbed and quartered
- 2 stalks celery
- 5 cups baby spinach

Directions

1. Add all the ingredients except vegetables/fruits first
2. Blend until smooth
3. Add the vegetable/fruits
4. Blend until smooth
5. Add a few ice cubes and serve the smoothie

Nutrition Values

- Calories: 172
- Fat: 1g
- Carbohydrates: 42g
- Protein: 3g

10. Cinnamon And Beet Booster Dose

Serving: 2

Prep Time: 5 minutes

Ingredients

- ¼ teaspoon cinnamon
- 1 medium cucumber, diced
- 1 medium beet, scrubbed and halved
- 1 cup kale, chopped
- 2 cups baby spinach, chopped

Directions

1. Add all the ingredients except vegetables/fruits first
2. Blend until smooth
3. Add the vegetable/fruits
4. Blend until smooth
5. Add a few ice cubes and serve the smoothie

Nutrition Values

- Calories: 134
- Fat: 5g
- Carbohydrates: 17g
- Protein: 7g

Chapter 2: Smoothies That Nourish Your Brain

11. The Wisest Watermelon Glass

Serving: 2

Prep Time: 5 minutes

Ingredients

- 1 tablespoon chia seeds
- 1 cup plain coconut yogurt
- 1 cup frozen cauliflower, riced
- 1 cup of frozen strawberries
- 1 cup coconut milk, unsweetened
- 1 and ½ cups watermelon, chopped

Directions

1. Add all the ingredients except vegetables/fruits first
2. Blend until smooth
3. Add the vegetable/fruits
4. Blend until smooth
5. Add a few ice cubes and serve the smoothie

Nutrition Values

- Calories: 130
- Fat: 2g
- Carbohydrates: 22g
- Protein: 8g

12. Cheery Charlie Checker

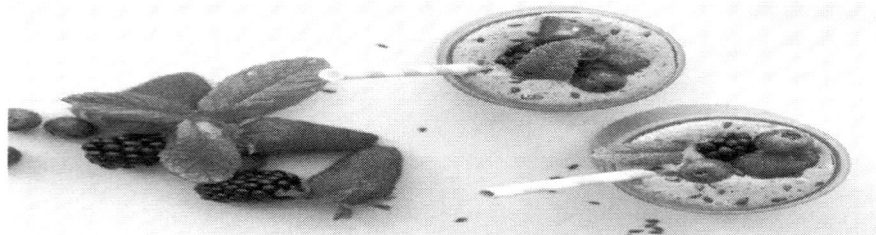

Serving: 2

Prep Time: 5 minutes

Ingredients

- 1 cup skim milk
- 1 cup frozen blueberries
- 1 fresh banana
- ¾ cup plain low-fat Greek yogurt
- ½ cup frozen cherries
- ½ cup of frozen strawberries
- 1 tablespoon chia seeds

Directions

1. Add all the ingredients except vegetables/fruits first
2. Blend until smooth
3. Add the vegetable/fruits
4. Blend until smooth
5. Add a few ice cubes and serve the smoothie

Nutrition Values

- Calories: 162
- Fat: 1g
- Carbohydrates: 33g
- Protein: 8g

13. The Pom Drink

Serving: 2

Prep Time: 5 minutes

Ingredients

- 1 cup plain coconut yogurt
- 1 cup baby spinach
- 1 cup frozen raspberries
- 1 cup frozen blackberries
- 1 cup unsweetened vanilla coconut milk

Directions

1. Add all the ingredients except vegetables/fruits first
2. Blend until smooth
3. Add the vegetable/fruits
4. Blend until smooth
5. Add a few ice cubes and serve the smoothie

Nutrition Values

- Calories: 148
- Fat: 0g
- Carbohydrates: 16g
- Protein: 0g

14.   Bright Rainbow Health

Serving: 2

Prep Time: 5 minutes

Ingredients

- 1 tablespoon hemp seeds
- ¼ cup pomegranate arils
- 1 cup plain Low-Fat Greek Yogurt
- 1 cup frozen tropical fruit mix
- 1 cup of frozen strawberries
- 1 cup unsweetened vanilla almond milk

Directions

1. Add all the ingredients except vegetables/fruits first
2. Blend until smooth
3. Add the vegetable/fruits
4. Blend until smooth
5. Add a few ice cubes and serve the smoothie

Nutrition Values

- Calories: 438
- Fat: 11g
- Carbohydrates: 91g
- Protein: 7g

15. Great Nutty Lion

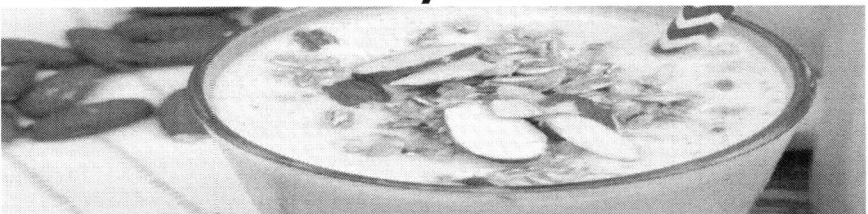

Serving: 2

Prep Time: 5 minutes

Ingredients

- 1 tablespoon almond butter
- 1 tablespoon chia seeds
- 4 ice cubes
- ¾ cup plain low-fat Greek yogurt
- 1 cup baby spinach
- 1 cup unsweetened almond milk
- 2 fresh bananas

Directions

1. Add all the ingredients except vegetables/fruits first
2. Blend until smooth
3. Add the vegetable/fruits
4. Blend until smooth
5. Add a few ice cubes and serve the smoothie

Nutrition Values

- Calories: 250
- Fat: 10g
- Carbohydrates: 51g
- Protein: 8g

16.   A Whole Melon Surprise

Serving: 2

Prep Time: 5 minutes

Ingredients

- 1 tablespoon chia seeds
- 4 ice cubes
- 1 fresh banana
- 1 cup cantaloupe
- 1 cup honeydew
- 1 cup plain coconut yogurt
- 1 cup unsweetened coconut milk

Directions

1. Add all the ingredients except vegetables/fruits first
2. Blend until smooth
3. Add the vegetable/fruits
4. Blend until smooth
5. Add a few ice cubes and serve the smoothie

Nutrition Values

- Calories: 134
- Fat: 2g
- Carbohydrates: 29g
- Protein: 3g

17. Muscular Macho Green

Serving: 2

Prep Time: 5 minutes

Ingredients

- 2 teaspoons matcha powder
- 1 tablespoon chia seeds
- ¾ cup plain coconut yogurt
- 1 fresh banana
- 1 cup baby spinach
- 1 cup of frozen mango
- 1 cup unsweetened coconut milk

Directions

1. Add all the ingredients except vegetables/fruits first
2. Blend until smooth
3. Add the vegetable/fruits
4. Blend until smooth
5. Add a few ice cubes and serve the smoothie

Nutrition Values

- Calories: 200
- Fat: 5g
- Carbohydrates: 35g
- Protein: 6g

18.   Buddha's Banana Berry

Serving: 2

Prep Time: 5 minutes

Ingredients

- 1 tablespoon hemp seeds
- ¾ cup plain low-fat Greek yogurt
- 1 fresh banana
- 1 cup baby spinach
- 1 cup frozen raspberries
- 1 cup unsweetened vanilla almond milk

Directions

1. Add all the ingredients except vegetables/fruits first
2. Blend until smooth
3. Add the vegetable/fruits
4. Blend until smooth
5. Add a few ice cubes and serve the smoothie

Nutrition Values

- Calories: 205
- Fat: 1g
- Carbohydrates: 51g
- Protein: 3g

19. Brain Nutrition-Analyzer

Serving: 2

Prep Time: 5 minutes

Ingredients

- 4 large ice cubes
- ¾ cup plain-low-fat Greek yogurt
- 1 cup baby spinach
- 1 cup unsweetened vanilla almond milk
- 2 fresh bananas
- 1 tablespoon almond butter
- 1 tablespoon peanut butter

Directions

1. Add all the ingredients except vegetables/fruits first
2. Blend until smooth
3. Add the vegetable/fruits
4. Blend until smooth
5. Add a few ice cubes and serve the smoothie

Nutrition Values

- Calories: 147
- Fat: 7g
- Carbohydrates: 21g
- Protein: 4g

20. Complete Banana Meal

Serving: 2

Prep Time: 5 minutes

Ingredients

- 1 tablespoon cacao powder
- 4 tablespoons chocolate hemp protein powder
- 1 fresh banana
- 1 cup baby spinach
- 1 cup of frozen coconut pieces
- 1 cup unsweetened vanilla almond milk

Directions

1. Add all the ingredients except vegetables/fruits first
2. Blend until smooth
3. Add the vegetable/fruits
4. Blend until smooth
5. Add a few ice cubes and serve the smoothie

Nutrition Values

- Calories: 234
- Fat: 10g
- Carbohydrates: 29g
- Protein: 13g

Chapter 3: Alkalizing Smoothies Protect Your Boned And Kidneys

21. Smoothie Vegetable Blast

Serving: 2

Prep Time: 5 minutes

Ingredients

- 1 cucumber, peeled and sliced
- 4 tomatoes, peeled
- 1 garlic clove
- ½ onion
- ½ cup rosemary infusion cooled
- Pepper and salt to taste
- 1 tablespoon virgin olive oil
- 1 cup kale
- 1 lemon, juiced

Directions

1. Add all the ingredients except vegetables/fruits first
2. Blend until smooth
3. Add the vegetable/fruits
4. Blend until smooth
5. Add a few ice cubes and serve the smoothie
6. Enjoy!

Nutrition Values

- Calories: 88
- Fat: 1g
- Carbohydrates: 21g
- Protein: 2g

22. Strawberry Banana Yogurt Smoothie

Serving: 2

Prep Time: 5 minutes

Ingredients

- 4 large strawberries
- ½ banana, sliced
- ½ cup blueberries
- 3 ounces soy yogurt
- 1 cup unsweetened soy milk
- 12 raw almonds
- 3 ice cubes

Directions

1. Add all the ingredients except vegetables/fruits first
2. Blend until smooth
3. Add the vegetable/fruits
4. Blend until smooth
5. Add a few ice cubes and serve the smoothie

Nutrition Values

- Calories: 200
- Fat: 2g
- Carbohydrates: 33g
- Protein: 13g

23. Cantaloupe Lettuce Smoothie

Serving: 2

Prep Time: 5 minutes

Ingredients

- 10 large romaine lettuce leaves
- 2 cups cantaloupe slice, chopped
- 1 cup strawberries, frozen
- 6 ice cubes

Directions

1. Add all the ingredients except vegetables/fruits first
2. Blend until smooth
3. Add the vegetable/fruits
4. Blend until smooth
5. Add a few ice cubes and serve the smoothie

Nutrition Values

- Calories: 209
- Fat: 1g
- Carbohydrates: 41g
- Protein: 12g

24.   Powerful Alkaline Smoothie

Serving: 2

Prep Time: 5 minutes

Ingredients

- 1 cup full-fat coconut milk
- 1 avocado, diced
- ½ cucumber, sliced
- 1 handful shake, chopped
- ½ inch ginger knob
- 1 tablespoon almond butter
- 1 tablespoon flaxseed
- 1 tablespoon coconut oil

Directions

1. Add all the ingredients except vegetables/fruits first
2. Blend until smooth
3. Add the vegetable/fruits
4. Blend until smooth
5. Add a few ice cubes and serve the smoothie

Nutrition Values

- Calories: 230
- Fat: 10g
- Carbohydrates: 38g
- Protein: 4g

25. Alkaline Breakfast Breaker

Serving: 2

Prep Time: 5 minutes

Ingredients

- 1 cup of coconut milk
- ¾ cup of filtered water
- 1 tablespoon coconut oil
- 1 handful of almonds
- 1 handful cashews
- 1 handful flaxseeds
- ½ avocado, diced
- 1 cucumber, sliced
- 1 handful kale, chopped

Directions

1. Add all the ingredients except vegetables/fruits first
2. Blend until smooth
3. Add the vegetable/fruits
4. Blend until smooth
5. Add a few ice cubes and serve the smoothie

Nutrition Values

- Calories: 414
- Fat: 33g
- Carbohydrates: 32g
- Protein: 8g

26. Mixed Berry Smoothie

Serving: 2

Prep Time: 5 minutes

Ingredients

- 2 cups of filtered water
- 1 teaspoon organic stevia powder
- 1 handful wild arugula
- ½ cup organic Greek yogurt, non-fat
- 1 banana, in frozen chunks
- 2 cups mixed berries

Directions

1. Add all the ingredients except vegetables/fruits first
2. Blend until smooth
3. Add the vegetable/fruits
4. Blend until smooth
5. Add a few ice cubes and serve the smoothie

Nutrition Values

- Calories: 222
- Fat: 2g
- Carbohydrates: 46g
- Protein: 8g

27. Sweet Kale Smoothie

Serving: 2

Prep Time: 5 minutes

Ingredients

- 2 cups kale leaves
- 1 ripe pear, peeled, cored, and chopped
- 15 green grapes
- 6 ounces fat-free plain Greek yogurt
- 2 tablespoons avocado, chopped
- 1-2 tablespoons fresh lime juice

Directions

1. Add all the ingredients except vegetables/fruits first
2. Blend until smooth
3. Add the vegetable/fruits
4. Blend until smooth
5. Add a few ice cubes and serve the smoothie

Nutrition Values

- Calories: 143
- Fat: 1g
- Carbohydrates: 36g
- Protein: 2g

28. Almond Butter Berry Smoothie

Serving: 2

Prep Time: 5 minutes

Ingredients

- 2 cups kale, chopped
- 2 cups almond milk, unsweetened
- 1 cup grapes, mixed
- 1 banana, peeled and frozen
- 4 tablespoons almond butter, raw
- 1 tablespoon chia

Directions

1. Add all the ingredients except vegetables/fruits first
2. Blend until smooth
3. Add the vegetable/fruits
4. Blend until smooth
5. Add a few ice cubes and serve the smoothie
6. Enjoy!

Nutrition Values

- Calories: 603
- Fat: 16g
- Carbohydrates: 65g
- Protein: 56g

29. Green Smoothie Bowl

Serving: 2

Prep Time: 5 minutes

Ingredients

- 1 ripe avocado, peeled and cut into cubes
- 1 cup of coconut water
- 1 small cucumber, cut in cubes
- 1 cup collard greens
- 1 small bunch fresh parsley
- 1 lime, juiced only
- 1 teaspoon chia seeds
- 1 tablespoon unsweetened coconut
- 1 tablespoon almond flakes

Directions

1. Add all the ingredients except vegetables/fruits first
2. Blend until smooth
3. Add the vegetable/fruits
4. Blend until smooth
5. Add a few ice cubes and serve the smoothie

Nutrition Values

- Calories: 180
- Fat: 7g
- Carbohydrates: 30g
- Protein: 4g

30. The Flat Belly Smoothie

Serving: 2

Prep Time: 5 minutes

Ingredients

- 3 ounces vanilla nonfat Greek yogurt
- 1 tablespoon almond butter
- ½ cup frozen blueberries
- ½ cup frozen pineapple
- 1 cup kale
- ¾ cup of water

Directions

1. Add all the ingredients except vegetables/fruits first
2. Blend until smooth
3. Add the vegetable/fruits
4. Blend until smooth
5. Add a few ice cubes and serve the smoothie

Nutrition Values

- Calories: 240
- Fat: 10g
- Carbohydrates: 30g
- Protein: 14g

Chapter 4: Anti-Aging Smoothies

31. Mango And Blueberry Bean Smoothie

Serving: 2

Prep Time: 5 minutes

Ingredients

- 1 teaspoon ground flaxseed
- 2 tablespoons almonds
- ¼ cup kidney beans
- ½ frozen bananas, sliced into rounds
- ½ cup of frozen mango
- ½ cup frozen blueberries
- 1 cup baby spinach
- ½ cup Greek yogurt
- ¾ cup of water
- 1 cup ice

Directions

1. Add all the ingredients except vegetables/fruits first
2. Blend until smooth
3. Add the vegetable/fruits
4. Blend until smooth
5. Add a few ice cubes and serve the smoothie
6. Enjoy!

Nutrition Values

- Calories: 459
- Fat: 10g
- Carbohydrates: 73g
- Protein: 26g

32. Pineapple Green Anti-Ager

Serving: 2

Prep Time: 5 minutes

Ingredients

- ½ teaspoon fresh ginger, grated
- ¼ teaspoon turmeric
- 1 cup romaine lettuce
- ¼ cup avocado, chopped
- ½ frozen banana, sliced
- 1 cup frozen pineapple, chunks
- 1 cup unsweetened vanilla almond milk
- ½ tablespoon lime juice
- 2 tablespoons Brazil nuts
- 1 Medjool date, pitted
- 1 cup of water

Directions

1. Add all the ingredients except vegetables/fruits first
2. Blend until smooth
3. Add the vegetable/fruits
4. Blend until smooth
5. Add a few ice cubes and serve the smoothie

Nutrition Values

- Calories: 410
- Fat: 8g
- Carbohydrates: 83g
- Protein: 9g

33. Apple Cherry Pumpkin Tea

Serving: 2

Prep Time: 5 minutes

Ingredients

- ¼ cup almonds
- ¼ cup canned pumpkin
- 1 red apple, cored, peel on
- 1 cup frozen cherries
- 1 cup brewed and chilled rooibos tea
- 1 tablespoon coconut flour
- 1 serving pea protein
- ¼ teaspoon cinnamon
- 1 pitted Medjool date
- 1 cup ice

Directions

1. Add all the ingredients except vegetables/fruits first
2. Blend until smooth
3. Add the vegetable/fruits
4. Blend until smooth
5. Add a few ice cubes and serve the smoothie

Nutrition Values

- Calories: 534
- Fat: 2g
- Carbohydrates: 78g
- Protein: 33g

34. Beets And Berry Beauty Enhancer

Serving: 2

Prep Time: 5 minutes

Ingredients

- 1 teaspoon ginger, grated
- 2 tablespoons pumpkin seeds
- ¼ cup avocado, chopped
- ¼ cup beet, steamed and peeled
- 1/3 cup frozen strawberries
- 1/3 cup frozen raspberries
- 1/3 cup frozen blueberries
- ½ cup Greek yogurt
- ½ cup unsweetened almond milk

Directions

1. Add all the ingredients except vegetables/fruits first
2. Blend until smooth
3. Add the vegetable/fruits
4. Blend until smooth
5. Add a few ice cubes and serve the smoothie

Nutrition Values

- Calories: 418
- Fat: 20g
- Carbohydrates: 50g
- Protein: 17g

35. A Honeydew and Cucumber Medley

Serving: 2

Prep Time: 5 minutes

Ingredients

- 1 cup ice
- 1 Medjool date, pitted
- 1 tablespoon ground flaxseed
- 1 tablespoon coconut flour
- ½ lime, juiced
- 1 tablespoon fresh mint, chopped
- 1 cup honeydew
- 1 cup cucumber, chopped
- ¾ cup Greek yogurt

Directions

1. Add all the ingredients except vegetables/fruits first
2. Blend until smooth
3. Add the vegetable/fruits
4. Blend until smooth
5. Add a few ice cubes and serve the smoothie

Nutrition Values

- Calories: 334
- Fat: 7g
- Carbohydrates: 50g
- Protein: 20g

36. Natural Nectarine

Serving: 2

Prep Time: 5 minutes

Ingredients

- 1 cup ice
- Pinch of turmeric
- 1 teaspoon vanilla extract
- 1 tablespoon coconut flour
- ¼ cup Brazil nuts
- 2 cups baby spinach
- 1 nectarine, pit removed
- 1 cup seedless red grapes
- 1 cup of coconut water

Directions

1. Add all the ingredients except vegetables/fruits first
2. Blend until smooth
3. Add the vegetable/fruits
4. Blend until smooth
5. Add a few ice cubes and serve the smoothie

Nutrition Values

- Calories: 475
- Fat: 22g
- Carbohydrates: 53g
- Protein: 11g

37. Fine Tea Toner

Serving: 2

Prep Time: 5 minutes

Ingredients

- ½ cup edamame shelled
- 1 cup dandelion greens
- 1 green apple, cored and peel on
- ½ frozen banana, sliced
- 1 cup brewed and chilled green tea
- 2 tablespoons walnuts
- 1-2 pitted Medjool dates
- 1 cup ice

Directions

1. Add all the ingredients except vegetables/fruits first
2. Blend until smooth
3. Add the vegetable/fruits
4. Blend until smooth
5. Add a few ice cubes and serve the smoothie

Nutrition Values

- Calories: 490
- Fat: 14g
- Carbohydrates: 88g
- Protein: 15g

38. The Grapefruit Glow

Serving: 2

Prep Time: 5 minutes

Ingredients

- 1 cup ice
- 2 tablespoons hemp seeds
- Pinch of cinnamon
- 1 teaspoon vanilla extract
- ½ lime, peeled
- ½ cup fresh cilantro, chopped
- 1 small cucumber, sliced
- ½ cup frozen pineapple
- 1 pink grapefruit, peeled
- ½ cup silken tofu
- ½ cup 100% orange juice

Directions

1. Add all the ingredients except vegetables/fruits first
2. Blend until smooth
3. Add the vegetable/fruits
4. Blend until smooth
5. Add a few ice cubes and serve the smoothie

Nutrition Values

- Calories: 377
- Fat: 10g

- Carbohydrates: 61g
- Protein: 15g

39. The Anti-Aging Avocado

Serving: 2

Prep Time: 5 minutes

Ingredients

- 1 cup ice
- 1 teaspoon vanilla extract
- 1 teaspoon grapeseed oil
- ½ cup avocado, chopped
- ½ cup of frozen strawberries
- ½ cup frozen peaches, chopped
- ½ cup plain Greek yogurt
- ¼ cup 100% pomegranate juice

Directions

1. Add all the ingredients except vegetables/fruits first
2. Blend until smooth
3. Add the vegetable/fruits
4. Blend until smooth
5. Add a few ice cubes and serve the smoothie

Nutrition Values

- Calories: 447
- Fat: 23g
- Carbohydrates: 39g
- Protein: 22g

40. A Green Grape Shake

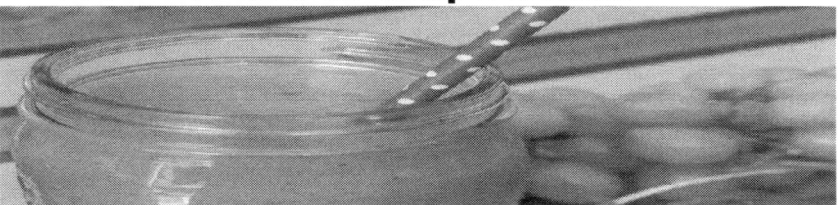

Serving: 2

Prep Time: 5 minutes

Ingredients

- 1 cup ice
- 2 tablespoons chia seeds
- 1 orange, peeled and quartered
- 1 pear, cored and chopped
- 1 cup green seedless grapes
- 2 cups baby kale
- ½ frozen banana, sliced
- ½ cup silken tofu
- ½ cup of water

Directions

1. Add all the ingredients except vegetables/fruits first
2. Blend until smooth
3. Add the vegetable/fruits
4. Blend until smooth
5. Add a few ice cubes and serve the smoothie

Nutrition Values

- Calories: 86
- Fat: 8g
- Carbohydrates: 3g
- Protein: 2g

Chapter 5: Anti-Oxidant Smoothies

41. Berry-Licious Anti-Oxidant Banana Smoothie

Serving: 2

Prep Time: 5 minutes

Ingredients

- 4 ice cubes
- 1 tablespoon protein powder
- 1 banana, cut in rounds
- 1 and ½ cups mixed berries of your choice
- 1 cup of coconut water, organic

Directions

1. Add all the ingredients except vegetables/fruits first
2. Blend until smooth
3. Add the vegetable/fruits
4. Blend until smooth

5. Add a few ice cubes and serve the smoothie
6. Enjoy!

Nutrition Values

- Calories: 465
- Fat: 8g
- Carbohydrates: 80g
- Protein: 8g

42. Protein-Packed Anti-Oxidizer

Serving: 2

Prep Time: 5 minutes

Ingredients

- 2/3 scoop protein powder
- 1 tablespoon chia seeds
- 1 tablespoon flaxseeds, ground
- ½ cup baby spinach
- ¼ banana, sliced
- 1 black plum
- 5 strawberries, frozen
- 1/3 cup blackberries, frozen
- 1/3 cup raspberries, frozen
- 1/3 cup blueberries, frozen
- 2/3 cup almond milk

Directions

1. Add all the ingredients except vegetables/fruits first

2. Blend until smooth
3. Add the vegetable/fruits
4. Blend until smooth
5. Add a few ice cubes and serve the smoothie
6. Enjoy!

Nutrition Values

- Calories: 190
- Fat: 2g
- Carbohydrates: 32g
- Protein: 14g

43. Triple Berry Supreme

Serving: 2

Prep Time: 5 minutes

Ingredients

- ½ cup almond milk
- ½ cup Greek yogurt, plain
- 1 tablespoon almond butter
- 1 tablespoon flaxseed meal
- 2 cups organic spinach
- 1 banana, frozen
- ¼ cup blueberries, frozen
- ½ cup raspberries, frozen
- ½ cup blackberries, frozen

Directions

1. Add all the ingredients except vegetables/fruits first
2. Blend until smooth
3. Add the vegetable/fruits
4. Blend until smooth
5. Add a few ice cubes and serve the smoothie

Nutrition Values

- Calories: 500
- Fat: 23g
- Carbohydrates: 58g
- Protein: 17g

44. A Green Grape Shake

Serving: 2

Prep Time: 5 minutes

Ingredients

- 1 cup ice
- 2 tablespoons chia seeds
- 1 orange, peeled and quartered
- 1 pear, cored and chopped
- 1 cup green seedless grapes
- 2 cups baby kale
- ½ frozen banana, sliced
- ½ cup silken tofu
- ½ cup of water

Directions

1. Add all the ingredients except vegetables/fruits first
2. Blend until smooth
3. Add the vegetable/fruits
4. Blend until smooth
5. Add a few ice cubes and serve the smoothie

Nutrition Values

- Calories: 429
- Fat: 13g
- Carbohydrates: 65g
- Protein: 21g

45. The Flaxseed Anti-Oxidizer

Serving: 2

Prep Time: 5 minutes

Ingredients

- 1 small banana
- 2 cups berries of your choice
- 2 packed cups of leafy greens of your choice
- 1 date, dried
- 1 teaspoon of cinnamon
- 2 ounces of green tea, brewed
- ¼ cup aloe vera gel
- 1 tablespoon of flaxseed
- ¼ teaspoon of pepper
- ¼ teaspoon of turmeric
- 1 tablespoon of Indian gooseberries, powdered
- 1 and ½ cup of almond milk

Directions

1. Add all the ingredients except vegetables/fruits first
2. Blend until smooth
3. Add the vegetable/fruits
4. Blend until smooth
5. Add a few ice cubes and serve the smoothie

Nutrition Values

- Calories: 110
- Fat: 3g
- Carbohydrates: 24g
- Protein: 2g

46. Mixed Berry and Kiwi Medley

Serving: 2

Prep Time: 5 minutes

Ingredients

- 1 small banana, cut into rounds
- 1 cup of orange juice
- 1 kiwi, skin removed
- 1 and ½ cups frozen berries, mixed

Directions

1. Add all the ingredients except vegetables/fruits first
2. Blend until smooth
3. Add the vegetable/fruits
4. Blend until smooth
5. Add a few ice cubes and serve the smoothie

Nutrition Values

- Calories: 345
- Fat: 2g
- Carbohydrates: 83g
- Protein: 6g

47. Supreme Green Tea Glass

Serving: 2

Prep Time: 5 minutes

Ingredients

- ½ teaspoon matcha powder
- 1 vanilla protein powder
- ¾ cup ice
- 1 cup strawberries, hulled
- 1 cup spinach leaves, loosely packed
- ½ banana, peeled
- 1 cup unsweetened almond milk

Directions

1. Add all the ingredients except vegetables/fruits first
2. Blend until smooth
3. Add the vegetable/fruits
4. Blend until smooth
5. Add a few ice cubes and serve the smoothie

Nutrition Values

- Calories: 233
- Fat: 2g
- Carbohydrates: 61g
- Protein: 2g

48.   Pomegranate Anti-Oxidizer

Serving: 2

Prep Time: 5 minutes

Ingredients

- 1 cup of water
- 1 cup unsweetened pomegranate juice
- 2 cups mixed berries, frozen

Directions

1. Add all the ingredients except vegetables/fruits first
2. Blend until smooth
3. Add the vegetable/fruits
4. Blend until smooth
5. Add a few ice cubes and serve the smoothie
6. Enjoy!

Nutrition Values

- Calories: 110
- Fat: 2g
- Carbohydrates: 20g
- Protein: 5g

49. Anti-Oxi Boosting Rolled Oats Smoothie

Serving: 2

Prep Time: 5 minutes

Ingredients

- 2 teaspoons LSA
- 2 tablespoons rolled oats
- 1 cup low-fat almond milk
- ½ a small banana, sliced into rounds
- ½ cup mixed berries

Directions

1. Add all the ingredients except vegetables/fruits first
2. Blend until smooth
3. Add the vegetable/fruits
4. Blend until smooth
5. Add a few ice cubes and serve the smoothie

Nutrition Values

- Calories: 342
- Fat: 4g
- Carbohydrates: 67g
- Protein: 15g

50. Anti-Oxi Rich Almond Flavored Smoothie

Serving: 2

Prep Time: 5 minutes

Ingredients

- Just a pinch of cinnamon
- ½ cup berries, frozen
- 1 banana, frozen
- 1 cup almond milk

Directions

1. Add all the ingredients except vegetables/fruits first
2. Blend until smooth
3. Add the vegetable/fruits
4. Blend until smooth
5. Add a few ice cubes and serve the smoothie

Nutrition Values

- Calories: 123
- Fat: 4g
- Carbohydrates: 20g
- Protein: 6g

Chapter 6: Cleansing Smoothies

51. A Melon Cucumber Medley

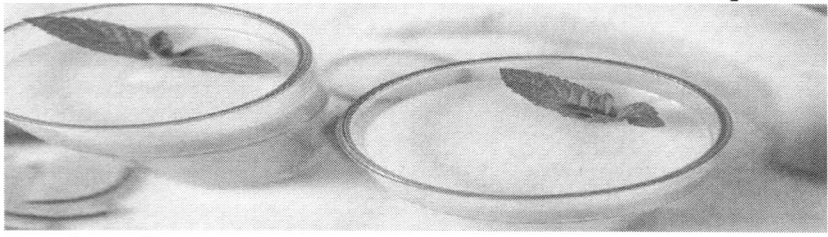

Serving: 2

Prep Time: 5 minutes

Ingredients

- ¾ cup honeydew melon, peeled and chopped
- 2 cups kale, chopped
- 1 medium cucumber, cubed

Directions

1. Add all the ingredients except vegetables/fruits first
2. Blend until smooth
3. Add the vegetable/fruits
4. Blend until smooth
5. Add a few ice cubes and serve the smoothie

Nutrition Values

- Calories: 112
- Fat: 2g
- Carbohydrates: 30g
- Protein: 2g

52.   Kale And Beet 2021 Fusion

Serving: 2

Prep Time: 5 minutes

Ingredients

- ¼ teaspoon cinnamon
- ¼ lemon, juiced
- 1 medium cucumber, cubed
- 4 cups kale, chopped
- 2 medium beets, scrubbed, halved

Directions

1. Add all the ingredients except vegetables/fruits first
2. Blend until smooth
3. Add the vegetable/fruits
4. Blend until smooth
5. Add a few ice cubes and serve the smoothie

Nutrition Values

- Calories: 69
- Fat: 0g
- Carbohydrates: 16g
- Protein: 4g

53. Strawberry And Watermelon Medley

Serving: 2

Prep Time: 5 minutes

Ingredients

- 1 cup ice
- 1 tablespoon fresh basil
- 1 cup watermelon, cubed
- 1 cup frozen strawberries, cubed
- 1 cup unsweetened almond milk

Directions

1. Add all the ingredients except vegetables/fruits first
2. Blend until smooth
3. Add the vegetable/fruits
4. Blend until smooth
5. Add a few ice cubes and serve the smoothie

Nutrition Values

- Calories: 130
- Fat: 9g
- Carbohydrates: 15g
- Protein: 3g

54. Punchy Watermelon

Serving: 2

Prep Time: 5 minutes

Ingredients

- 1 large cucumber, cubed
- 1 cup kale, chopped
- 1 cup baby spinach, chopped
- 4 cups watermelon, chopped

Directions

1. Add all the ingredients except vegetables/fruits first
2. Blend until smooth
3. Add the vegetable/fruits
4. Blend until smooth
5. Add a few ice cubes and serve the smoothie
6. Enjoy!

Nutrition Values

- Calories: 464
- Fat: 20g
- Carbohydrates: 65g
- Protein: 23g

55. Hearty Cucumber Quencher

Serving: 2

Prep Time: 5 minutes

Ingredients

- 2 cups kale, chopped
- 1 fuji apple, quartered
- 1 large cucumber, cubed

Directions

1. Add all the ingredients except vegetables/fruits first
2. Blend until smooth
3. Add the vegetable/fruits
4. Blend until smooth
5. Add a few ice cubes and serve the smoothie

Nutrition Values

- Calories: 180
- Fat: 2g
- Carbohydrates: 40g
- Protein: 5g

56. Dandelion Aloha

Serving: 2

Prep Time: 5 minutes

Ingredients

- 1 cup ice
- 1 cup pineapple, chopped
- 2 cups dandelion greens
- 1 cup unsweetened almond milk

Directions

1. Add all the ingredients except vegetables/fruits first
2. Blend until smooth
3. Add the vegetable/fruits
4. Blend until smooth
5. Add a few ice cubes and serve the smoothie

Nutrition Values

- Calories: 121
- Fat: 5g
- Carbohydrates: 18g
- Protein: 1g

57. Blueberry Detox Drink

Serving: 2

Prep Time: 5 minutes

Ingredients

- 1 cup ice
- 2 tablespoons spirulina
- ½ frozen banana, sliced
- 2 cups blueberries, frozen
- 2 cups baby spinach
- 2 cups of coconut water

Directions

1. Add all the ingredients except vegetables/fruits first
2. Blend until smooth
3. Add the vegetable/fruits
4. Blend until smooth
5. Add a few ice cubes and serve the smoothie

Nutrition Values

- Calories: 685
- Fat: 60g
- Carbohydrates: 40g
- Protein: 32g

58. Cocoa Pumpkin

Serving: 2

Prep Time: 5 minutes

Ingredients

- ¼ teaspoon pumpkin spice
- 1 tablespoon maple syrup
- 2 tablespoons organic unsweetened cocoa powder
- ¼ frozen banana, sliced
- ½ Barlett pear, cored
- 3 cups baby spinach
- 1 cup organic pumpkin puree
- 1 cup unsweetened almond milk

Directions

1. Add all the ingredients except vegetables/fruits first
2. Blend until smooth
3. Add the vegetable/fruits
4. Blend until smooth
5. Add a few ice cubes and serve the smoothie

Nutrition Values

- Calories: 486
- Fat: 28g
- Carbohydrates: 64g
- Protein: 11g

59. Twisty Cucumber Honeydew

Serving: 2

Prep Time: 5 minutes

Ingredients

- 1 cup ice
- 1 tablespoon fresh mint
- 2 cucumbers, chopped
- 1 cup honeydew melon, peeled, seeded, and chopped
- 1 cup of coconut water

Directions

1. Add all the ingredients except vegetables/fruits first
2. Blend until smooth
3. Add the vegetable/fruits
4. Blend until smooth
5. Add a few ice cubes and serve the smoothie

Nutrition Values

- Calories: 70
- Fat: 1g
- Carbohydrates: 13g
- Protein: 2g

60. Chocolaty Pleasure Delight

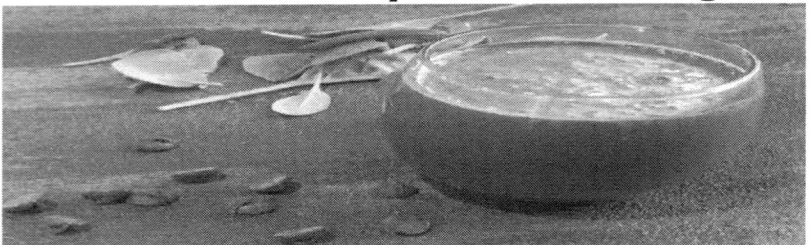

Serving: 2

Prep Time: 5 minutes

Ingredients

- 1 cup unsweetened coconut milk
- 1 cup ice
- 1 tablespoon pure maple syrup
- 1 tablespoon green superfood
- 2 tablespoon unsweetened cocoa powder
- ½ frozen bananas, sliced
- 2 cups baby spinach
- 1 cup unsweetened coconut milk

Directions

1. Add all the ingredients except vegetables/fruits first
2. Blend until smooth
3. Add the vegetable/fruits
4. Blend until smooth
5. Add a few ice cubes and serve the smoothie

Nutrition Values

- Calories: 306
- Fat: 8g
- Carbohydrates: 56g
- Protein: 10g

Chapter 7: Diabetic Smoothies

61. Berry-Licious Meta Booster

Serving: 2

Prep Time: 5 minutes

Ingredients

- ¼ cup garbanzo bean
- 1 teaspoon flax oil
- ½ cup frozen blueberries
- ½ cup frozen broccoli florets
- 6 ounces Greek yogurt
- ¾ cup brewed and chilled green tea

Directions

1. Add all the ingredients except vegetables/fruits first
2. Blend until smooth
3. Add the vegetable/fruits
4. Blend until smooth
5. Add a few ice cubes and serve the smoothie
6. Enjoy!

Nutrition Values

- Calories: 200
- Fat: 3g
- Carbohydrates: 41g
- Protein: 5g

62. Healthy Potato Pie Glass

Serving: 2

Prep Time: 5 minutes

Ingredients

- 1 cup ice
- ¼ teaspoon cinnamon
- ¼ cup rolled oats
- ½ frozen banana
- 1 small orange, peeled
- ½ cup sweet potato, cooked and peeled
- 6 ounces Greek yogurt
- ½ cup untweeted almond milk

Directions

1. Add all the ingredients except vegetables/fruits first
2. Blend until smooth
3. Add the vegetable/fruits
4. Blend until smooth
5. Add a few ice cubes and serve the smoothie

Nutrition Values

- Calories: 400
- Fat: 20g
- Carbohydrates: 41g
- Protein: 20g

63. Vegetable And Green Tea Smoothie

Serving: 2

Prep Time: 5 minutes

Ingredients

- 1 cup ice
- 2 tablespoons chia seeds
- ½ frozen bananas, diced
- ½ cup of frozen green peas
- ½ cup frozen cauliflower
- ½ cup frozen broccoli
- ¾ cup non-fat Greek yogurt
- 1 cup brewed and chilled green tea

Directions

1. Add all the ingredients except vegetables/fruits first
2. Blend until smooth
3. Add the vegetable/fruits
4. Blend until smooth
5. Add a few ice cubes and serve the smoothie

Nutrition Values

- Calories: 110
- Fat: 0g
- Carbohydrates: 23g
- Protein: 2g

64. Tropical Kiwi Pineapple

Serving: 2

Prep Time: 5 minutes

Ingredients

- 1 cup ice
- 1 tablespoon ground flaxseed
- 1 tablespoon psyllium husk
- 6 almonds
- 2 tablespoons unsweetened coconut
- 1 medium kiwi, skin intact

Directions

1. Add all the ingredients except vegetables/fruits first
2. Blend until smooth
3. Add the vegetable/fruits
4. Blend until smooth
5. Add a few ice cubes and serve the smoothie

Nutrition Values

- Calories: 300
- Fat: 15g
- Carbohydrates: 40g
- Protein: 1g

65. Greens And Herbs for All

Serving: 2

Prep Time: 5 minutes

Ingredients

- 1 cup ice
- 1 tablespoon ground flaxseed
- 1/3 cup fresh cilantro, chopped
- ½ lemon, juiced
- 1 pear, cored and chopped
- ½ frozen banana, sliced into rounds
- 2 cups baby spinach, chopped
- 2 stalks celery, chopped
- 1 cup romaine lettuce, chopped
- ½ cup non-fat Greek yogurt
- 1 cup of water

Directions

1. Add all the ingredients except vegetables/fruits first
2. Blend until smooth
3. Add the vegetable/fruits
4. Blend until smooth
5. Add a few ice cubes and serve the smoothie

Nutrition Values

- Calories: 184
- Fat: 1g
- Carbohydrates: 45g
- Protein: 6g

66. Avocado And Edamame Drink

Serving: 2

Prep Time: 5 minutes

Ingredients

- ¾ cup almond milk
- ½ cup edamame shelled
- ¼ cup avocado, diced
- ½ cup of frozen mango, diced
- 1 tablespoon coconut flour
- 1 cup ice

Directions

1. Add all the ingredients except vegetables/fruits first
2. Blend until smooth
3. Add the vegetable/fruits
4. Blend until smooth
5. Add a few ice cubes and serve the smoothie

Nutrition Values

- Calories: 245
- Fat: 15g
- Carbohydrates: 28g
- Protein: 4g

67. Peanut Butter and Cherry Delight

Serving: 2

Prep Time: 5 minutes

Ingredients

- 1 tablespoon psyllium husk
- 1 tablespoon unsweetened peanut butter
- 2 tablespoons powdered peanut butter
- ¾ cup frozen cherries
- ½ cup silken tofu
- ¾ cup non-fat milk such as almond milk

Directions

1. Add all the ingredients except vegetables/fruits first
2. Blend until smooth
3. Add the vegetable/fruits
4. Blend until smooth
5. Add a few ice cubes and serve the smoothie

Nutrition Values

- Calories: 170
- Fat: 8g
- Carbohydrates: 24g
- Protein: 6g

68. White Bean and Mango Delight

Serving: 2

Prep Time: 5 minutes

Ingredients

- 1 cup ice
- 2 tablespoons fresh mint leaves, chopped
- 1 tablespoon coconut flour
- 2 tablespoons hemp seeds
- ½ cup frozen spinach
- ½ cup of frozen mango
- 1/3 cup white beans, rinsed
- 1 cup cashew milk

Directions

1. Add all the ingredients except vegetables/fruits first
2. Blend until smooth
3. Add the vegetable/fruits
4. Blend until smooth
5. Add a few ice cubes and serve the smoothie

Nutrition Values

- Calories: 290
- Fat: 10g
- Carbohydrates: 37g
- Protein: 12g

69. Cashew Apple Glass

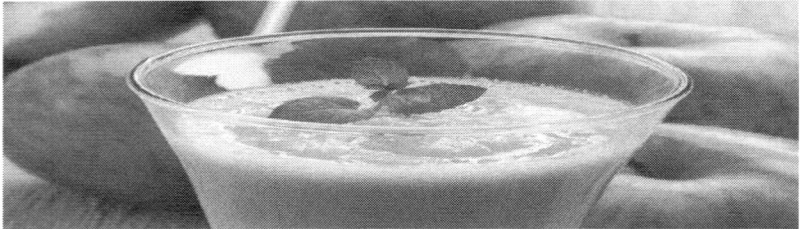

Serving: 2

Prep Time: 5 minutes

Ingredients

- 1 cup ice
- 1 teaspoon apple pie spice
- 1 tablespoon cashew butter
- 1 medium apple, peeled and chopped
- ½ cup frozen peaches
- 1 serving whey protein powder
- ¾ cup plain soymilk

Directions

1. Add all the ingredients except vegetables/fruits first
2. Blend until smooth
3. Add the vegetable/fruits
4. Blend until smooth
5. Add a few ice cubes and serve the smoothie

Nutrition Values

- Calories: 500
- Fat: 17g
- Carbohydrates: 63g
- Protein: 9g

70. Spicy Pear and Green Tea

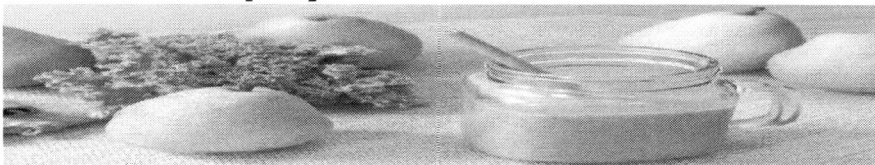

Serving: 2

Prep Time: 5 minutes

Ingredients

- 1 cup brewed and chilled green tea
- ½ cup silken tofu
- 1 small pear, skin on, cut into small pieces
- ½ frozen bananas, sliced into rounds
- 2 tablespoons ground flaxseed
- 1/8 teaspoon cayenne
- 2 tablespoons lemon juice
- ½ cup ice

Directions

1. Add all the ingredients except vegetables/fruits first
2. Blend until smooth
3. Add the vegetable/fruits
4. Blend until smooth
5. Add a few ice cubes and serve the smoothie

Nutrition Values

- Calories: 422
- Fat: 13g
- Carbohydrates: 51g
- Protein: 31g

Chapter 8: Digestive Health Smoothies

71. Tropical Storm Glass

Serving: 2

Prep Time: 5 minutes

Ingredients

- 1 tablespoon hemp seeds
- ¾ cup plain coconut yogurt
- 1 fresh banana
- 1 cup unsweetened coconut milk
- 1 and ½ cups frozen papaya blend (mix of papaya, mango, strawberry, and pineapple)

Directions

1. Add all the ingredients except vegetables/fruits first
2. Blend until smooth

3. Add the vegetable/fruits
4. Blend until smooth
5. Add a few ice cubes and serve the smoothie
6. Enjoy!

Nutrition Values

- Calories: 186
- Fat: 0g
- Carbohydrates: 14g
- Protein: 1g

72. Cool Strawberry 365

Serving: 2

Prep Time: 5 minutes

Ingredients

- 1 tablespoon chia seeds
- ½ cup of water
- ¾ cup Siggi's whole milk vanilla yogurt
- 1 cup frozen peaches
- 1 cup baby spinach
- 1 cup of frozen mixed berries
- 1 cup unsweetened vanilla almond milk

Directions

1. Add all the ingredients except vegetables/fruits first
2. Blend until smooth
3. Add the vegetable/fruits
4. Blend until smooth
5. Add a few ice cubes and serve the smoothie

Nutrition Values

- Calories: 167
- Fat: 6g
- Carbohydrates: 25g
- Protein: 8g

73. Noteworthy Vitamin C

Serving: 2

Prep Time: 5 minutes

Ingredients

- 1 tablespoon chia seeds
- 1 clementine
- ¾ cup plain low-fat Greek yogurt
- 1 cup of frozen strawberries
- 1 cup cantaloupe
- 1 cup unsweetened vanilla almond milk

Directions

1. Add all the ingredients except vegetables/fruits first
2. Blend until smooth
3. Add the vegetable/fruits
4. Blend until smooth
5. Add a few ice cubes and serve the smoothie

Nutrition Values

- Calories: 209
- Fat: 2g
- Carbohydrates: 41g
- Protein: 12g

74. Hearty Papaya Drink

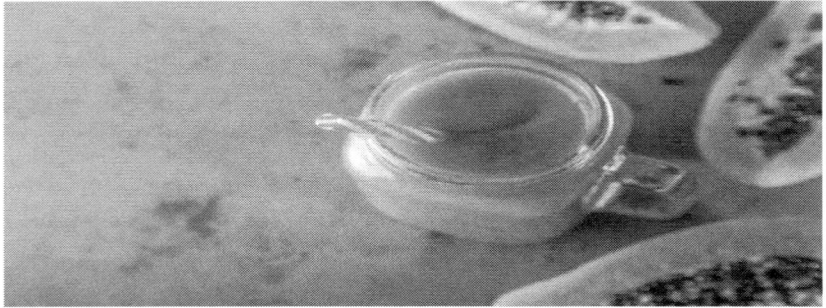

Serving: 2

Prep Time: 5 minutes

Ingredients

- 1 tablespoon chia seeds
- ¾ cup plain coconut yogurt
- 1 cup baby spinach
- 1 cup frozen papaya
- 1 cup frozen tropical fruit mix
- 1 cup coconut milk, unsweetened

Directions

1. Add all the ingredients except vegetables/fruits first
2. Blend until smooth
3. Add the vegetable/fruits
4. Blend until smooth
5. Add a few ice cubes and serve the smoothie

Nutrition Values

- Calories: 192
- Fat: 7g
- Carbohydrates: 31g
- Protein: 3g

75.   A Minty Drink

Serving: 2

Prep Time: 5 minutes

Ingredients

- 1 tablespoon hemp seeds
- Fresh mint leaves
- ¾ cup plain coconut yogurt
- 1 cup of frozen mango
- 1 cup of frozen strawberries
- 1 cup unsweetened vanilla almond milk

Directions

1. Add all the ingredients except vegetables/fruits first
2. Blend until smooth
3. Add the vegetable/fruits
4. Blend until smooth
5. Add a few ice cubes and serve the smoothie

Nutrition Values

- Calories: 391
- Fat: 10g
- Carbohydrates: 44g
- Protein: 5g

76. The Baked Apple

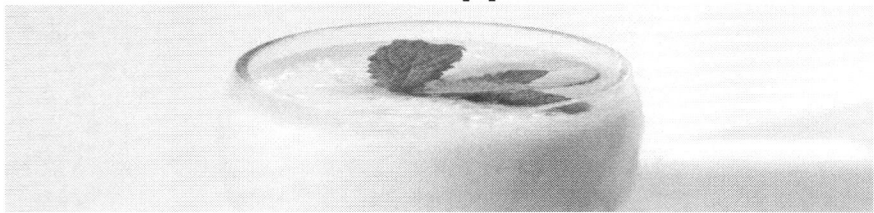

Serving: 2

Prep Time: 5 minutes

Ingredients

- Dash ground cinnamon
- 1 tablespoon rolled oats
- 1 tablespoon hemp seeds
- ¾ cup Siggi's Whole milk vanilla yogurt
- 1 cup pear chunks
- 1 cup apple chunks
- 1 cup unsweetened vanilla almond milk

Directions

1. Add all the ingredients except vegetables/fruits first
2. Blend until smooth
3. Add the vegetable/fruits
4. Blend until smooth
5. Add a few ice cubes and serve the smoothie

Nutrition Values

- Calories: 160
- Fat: 4g
- Carbohydrates: 33g
- Protein: 2g

77. The Amazing Acai

Serving: 2

Prep Time: 5 minutes

Ingredients

- 1 tablespoon hemp seeds
- 1 pack frozen acai
- 1 cup baby spinach
- ¾ cup plain coconut yogurt
- 1 fresh banana
- 1 cup unsweetened hemp milk

Directions

1. Add all the ingredients except vegetables/fruits first
2. Blend until smooth
3. Add the vegetable/fruits
4. Blend until smooth
5. Add a few ice cubes and serve the smoothie

Nutrition Values

- Calories: 225
- Fat: 8g
- Carbohydrates: 40g
- Protein: 4g

78. Fine Yō "Mama" Matcha

Serving: 2

Prep Time: 5 minutes

Ingredients

- 2 teaspoons matcha powder
- 1 tablespoon hemp seeds
- ¾ cup of coconut yogurt
- 1 fresh banana
- 1 cup frozen pineapple
- 1 cup unsweetened almond milk

Directions

1. Add all the ingredients except vegetables/fruits first
2. Blend until smooth
3. Add the vegetable/fruits
4. Blend until smooth
5. Add a few ice cubes and serve the smoothie

Nutrition Values

- Calories: 216
- Fat: 1g
- Carbohydrates: 52g
- Protein: 3g

79. The Pumpkin Eye

Serving: 2

Prep Time: 5 minutes

Ingredients

- Dash of ground cinnamon
- 1 tablespoon hemp seeds
- ½ cup unsweetened hemp milk
- ¾ cup Siggi's whole milk vanilla yogurt
- 1 fresh banana
- 1 cup kale
- 1 cup pure canned pumpkin

Directions

1. Add all the ingredients except vegetables/fruits first
2. Blend until smooth
3. Add the vegetable/fruits
4. Blend until smooth
5. Add a few ice cubes and serve the smoothie

Nutrition Values

- Calories: 216
- Fat: 3g
- Carbohydrates: 48g
- Protein: 3g

80. Great Green Garden

Serving: 2

Prep Time: 5 minutes

Ingredients

- 1 teaspoon spirulina
- Few fresh mint leaves
- ½ cup cucumber, peeled
- ¾ cup plain coconut yogurt
- 1 cup pineapple, frozen
- 1 cup mango, frozen
- 1 cup unsweetened coconut milk

Directions

1. Add all the ingredients except vegetables/fruits first
2. Blend until smooth
3. Add the vegetable/fruits
4. Blend until smooth
5. Add a few ice cubes and serve the smoothie

Nutrition Values

- Calories: 200
- Fat: 6g
- Carbohydrates: 32g
- Protein: 10g

Chapter 9: High-Energy Smoothies

81. Generous Mango Surprise

Serving: 2

Prep Time: 5 minutes

Ingredients

- 1 tablespoon spirulina
- 3 cups froze mango, sliced
- 1 and ½ cups kale
- 2 and ½ cups unsweetened almond milk

Directions

1. Add all the ingredients except vegetables/fruits first
2. Blend until smooth
3. Add the vegetable/fruits
4. Blend until smooth
5. Add a few ice cubes and serve the smoothie

Nutrition Values

- Calories: 72
- Fat: 0g
- Carbohydrates: 17g
- Protein: 1g

82. Powerful Purple Smoothie

Serving: 2

Prep Time: 5 minutes

Ingredients

- 1 tablespoon green superfood as you like
- 1 tablespoon spirulina
- 1 frozen banana, sliced
- 2 acai frozen berry packs
- 2 cups baby spinach
- 1 and ¼ cups of coconut water

Directions

1. Add all the ingredients except vegetables/fruits first
2. Blend until smooth
3. Add the vegetable/fruits
4. Blend until smooth
5. Add a few ice cubes and serve the smoothie

Nutrition Values

- Calories: 70
- Fat: 2g
- Carbohydrates: 14g
- Protein: 3g

83. Banana Apple Blast

Serving: 2

Prep Time: 5 minutes

Ingredients

- 1 cup ice
- 1 teaspoon bee pollen
- 1 teaspoon spirulina
- 1 cup fresh pineapple, sliced
- 1 frozen banana, sliced
- 2 cups baby spinach
- 1 and ½ cups unsweetened coconut milk drink

Directions

1. Add all the ingredients except vegetables/fruits first
2. Blend until smooth
3. Add the vegetable/fruits
4. Blend until smooth
5. Add a few ice cubes and serve the smoothie

Nutrition Values

- Calories: 209
- Fat: 2g
- Carbohydrates: 51g
- Protein: 2g

84. Energizing Pineapple Kicker

Serving: 2

Prep Time: 5 minutes

Ingredients

- 1 medium cucumber, diced
- ¾ cup fresh pineapple
- 1 tablespoon fresh ginger
- 3 cups baby spinach

Directions

1. Add all the ingredients except vegetables/fruits first
2. Blend until smooth
3. Add the vegetable/fruits
4. Blend until smooth
5. Add a few ice cubes and serve the smoothie

Nutrition Values

- Calories: 236
- Fat: 6g
- Carbohydrates: 46g
- Protein: 4g

85. Dandelion And Carrot Booster

Serving: 2

Prep Time: 5 minutes

Ingredients

- ½ fuji apple
- 1 tablespoon fresh ginger
- ½ pound organic carrots, scrubbed
- ¾ cup dandelion greens
- 2 cups baby spinach

Directions

1. Add all the ingredients except vegetables/fruits first
2. Blend until smooth
3. Add the vegetable/fruits
4. Blend until smooth
5. Add a few ice cubes and serve the smoothie

Nutrition Values

- Calories: 160
- Fat: 5g
- Carbohydrates: 30g
- Protein: 5g

86. Green Skinny Energizer

Serving: 2

Prep Time: 5 minutes

Ingredients

- ½ ripe mango, pitted and sliced
- 1 cup kale, chopped
- 3 cups baby spinach
- 1 cup of coconut water

Directions

1. Add all the ingredients except vegetables/fruits first
2. Blend until smooth
3. Add the vegetable/fruits
4. Blend until smooth
5. Add a few ice cubes and serve the smoothie
6. Enjoy!

Nutrition Values

- Calories: 300
- Fat: 13g
- Carbohydrates: 37g
- Protein: 10g

87. Awesome Pineapple and Carrot Blend

Serving: 2

Prep Time: 5 minutes

Ingredients

- 1/8 teaspoon cinnamon
- 1 cup fresh pineapple
- 3 organic carrots, scrubbed and sliced
- 5 cups baby spinach
- 1 large cucumber, diced

Directions

1. Add all the ingredients except vegetables/fruits first
2. Blend until smooth
3. Add the vegetable/fruits
4. Blend until smooth
5. Add a few ice cubes and serve the smoothie

Nutrition Values

- Calories: 82
- Fat: 0g
- Carbohydrates: 21g
- Protein: 1g

88. Mango Energizer

Serving: 2

Prep Time: 5 minutes

Ingredients

- 4 tablespoon protein powder
- 2 teaspoons spirulina
- 1 teaspoon bee pollen
- 1 frozen banana, sliced
- 1 cup of frozen mango, sliced
- 2 cups baby spinach
- 1 and ¼ cup unsweetened almond milk

Directions

1. Add all the ingredients except vegetables/fruits first
2. Blend until smooth
3. Add the vegetable/fruits
4. Blend until smooth
5. Add a few ice cubes and serve the smoothie

Nutrition Values

- Calories: 136
- Fat: 2g
- Carbohydrates: 29g
- Protein: 5g

89. Powerful Green Frenzy

Serving: 2

Prep Time: 5 minutes

Ingredients

- 1 cup ice
- 2 tablespoons almond butter
- 1 teaspoon spirulina
- 3 teaspoon fresh ginger
- 1 and ½ frozen bananas, sliced
- 2 cups baby spinach, chopped
- 1 cup kale
- 1 and ½ cups unsweetened almond milk

Directions

1. Add all the ingredients except vegetables/fruits first
2. Blend until smooth
3. Add the vegetable/fruits
4. Blend until smooth
5. Add a few ice cubes and serve the smoothie

Nutrition Values

- Calories: 350
- Fat: 4g
- Carbohydrates: 54g
- Protein: 30g

Chapter 10: Green Smoothies Recipes

90. The Minty Cucumber

Serving: 2

Prep Time: 5 minutes

Ingredients

- ½ cup ice
- 1 and ½ cups swiss chard, chopped
- ¾ cup cucumber, diced
- 1 pear, roughly chopped
- ¼ cup fresh cilantro, chopped
- 4 fresh mint leaves, chopped
- ½ lemon, juiced
- ¼ cup of water

Directions

1. Add all the ingredients except vegetables/fruits first

2. Blend until smooth
3. Add the vegetable/fruits
4. Blend until smooth
5. Add a few ice cubes and serve the smoothie
6. Enjoy

Nutrition Values

- Calories: 105
- Fat: 0g
- Carbohydrates: 25g
- Protein: 3g

91. Lemon Cilantro Delight

Serving: 2

Prep Time: 5 minutes

Ingredients

- ½ cup ice
- 1 cup dandelion greens, chopped
- 2 celery stalks, roughly chopped
- 1 pear, roughly chopped
- 1 tablespoon chia seeds
- ¼ cup fresh cilantro, chopped
- Juice of ½ lemon
- ¼ cup of water

Directions

1. Add all the ingredients except vegetables/fruits first
2. Blend until smooth
3. Add the vegetable/fruits
4. Blend until smooth
5. Add a few ice cubes and serve the smoothie

Nutrition Values

- Calories: 200
- Fat: 5g
- Carbohydrates: 34g
- Protein: 5g

92. A Peachy Medley

Serving: 2

Prep Time: 5 minutes

Ingredients

- 1 cup of coconut water
- 1 tablespoon flaxseed, ground
- 1 scoop vanilla protein powder
- ¼ cup frozen peaches
- ½ cup frozen tart cherries
- 1 cup dandelion greens, chopped

Directions

1. Add all the ingredients except vegetables/fruits first
2. Blend until smooth
3. Add the vegetable/fruits
4. Blend until smooth
5. Add a few ice cubes and serve the smoothie

Nutrition Values

- Calories: 300
- Fat: 7g
- Carbohydrates: 45g
- Protein: 32g

93. Cilantro And Citrus Glass

Serving: 2

Prep Time: 5 minutes

- ½ cup ice
- 2 cups arugula
- ½ cup celery, diced
- 1 grapefruit, peeled and segmented
- 1 handful fresh cilantro leaves, chopped
- ½ lemon, juiced
- ½ cup of water

Directions

1. Add all the ingredients except vegetables/fruits first
2. Blend until smooth
3. Add the vegetable/fruits
4. Blend until smooth
5. Add a few ice cubes and serve the smoothie

Nutrition Values

- Calories: 75
- Fat: 1g
- Carbohydrates: 16g
- Protein: 3g

94. The Deep Green Lagoon

Serving: 2

Prep Time: 5 minutes

Ingredients

- ½ cup ice
- ½ cup collard greens, chopped
- 1 cup spinach, chopped
- ½ cup fresh broccoli florets, diced
- 1 pear, roughly chopped
- 1 teaspoon spirulina powder
- ½ cup of water

Directions

1. Add all the ingredients except vegetables/fruits first
2. Blend until smooth
3. Add the vegetable/fruits
4. Blend until smooth
5. Add a few ice cubes and serve the smoothie
6. Enjoy!

Nutrition Values

- Calories: 124
- Fat: 1g
- Carbohydrates: 30g
- Protein: 4g

95. The Wild Matcha Delight

Serving: 2

Prep Time: 5 minutes

Ingredients

- 1 cup unsweetened coconut milk
- 1 teaspoon matcha powder
- ½ teaspoon cinnamon
- 1 cup baby spinach, chopped
- 1 cup wild blueberries, frozen

Directions

1. Add all the ingredients except vegetables/fruits first
2. Blend until smooth
3. Add the vegetable/fruits
4. Blend until smooth
5. Add a few ice cubes and serve the smoothie
6. Enjoy!

Nutrition Values

- Calories: 130
- Fat: 3g
- Carbohydrates: 21g
- Protein: 5g

96. The Green Potato Chai

Serving: 2

Prep Time: 5 minutes

Ingredients

- ½ cup chilled, brewed chai
- ½ cup ice
- 1 and ½ cups kale, chopped
- 1 pear, roughly chopped
- 1 scoop unsweetened protein powder
- ¼ teaspoon cinnamon

Directions

1. Add all the ingredients except vegetables/fruits first
2. Blend until smooth
3. Add the vegetable/fruits
4. Blend until smooth
5. Add a few ice cubes and serve the smoothie

Nutrition Values

- Calories: 286
- Fat: 1g
- Carbohydrates: 43g
- Protein: 29g

97. Lemon Cilantro Delight

Serving: 2

Prep Time: 5 minutes

Ingredients

- ½ cup ice
- 1 cup dandelion greens, chopped
- 2 celery stalks, roughly chopped
- 1 pear, roughly chopped
- 1 tablespoon chia seeds
- ¼ cup fresh cilantro, chopped
- Juice of ½ lemon
- ¼ cup of water

Directions

1. Add all the ingredients except vegetables/fruits first
2. Blend until smooth
3. Add the vegetable/fruits
4. Blend until smooth
5. Add a few ice cubes and serve the smoothie

Nutrition Values

- Calories: 200
- Fat: 11g
- Carbohydrates: 27g
- Protein: 4g

98. Lovely Green Gazpacho

Serving: 2

Prep Time: 5 minutes

Ingredients

- ½ cup ice
- 1 cup collard greens, chopped
- ¼ cup red bell pepper, diced
- ½ cup frozen broccoli florets
- ½ cup fresh tomatoes, chopped
- 1 garlic clove
- ¼ cup fresh cilantro, chopped
- ½ a lemon, juiced
- ½ cup of water

Directions

1. Add all the ingredients except vegetables/fruits first
2. Blend until smooth
3. Add the vegetable/fruits
4. Blend until smooth
5. Add a few ice cubes and serve the smoothie

Nutrition Values

- Calories: 70
- Fat: 1g
- Carbohydrates: 13g
- Protein: 4g

99. Tropical Matcha Kale

Serving: 2

Prep Time: 5 minutes

Ingredients

- ½ cup ice
- 1 cup kale, chopped
- ½ cup of frozen mango died
- 1 teaspoon matcha powder
- ½ cup plain kefir
- ¼ cup of cold water

Directions

1. Add all the ingredients except vegetables/fruits first
2. Blend until smooth
3. Add the vegetable/fruits
4. Blend until smooth
5. Add a few ice cubes and serve the smoothie

Nutrition Values

- Calories: 126
- Fat: 2g
- Carbohydrates: 23g
- Protein: 6g

Chapter 11: Healthful Skin Recipes
100. Evergreen Morning Dew

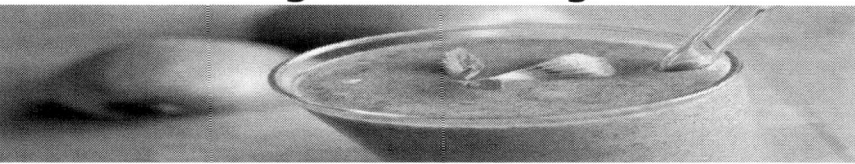

Serving: 2

Prep Time: 5 minutes

Ingredients

- ½ cup ice
- 1 cup kale, chopped
- 1 large red bell pepper, diced
- 1 large kiwi, peeled
- 1 scoop collagen protein powder
- Pinch of cayenne
- ½ lemon, juice
- ½ cup of water

Directions

1. Add all the ingredients except vegetables/fruits first
2. Blend until smooth
3. Add the vegetable/fruits
4. Blend until smooth
5. Add a few ice cubes and serve the smoothie

Nutrition Values

- Calories: 157
- Fat: 1g
- Carbohydrates: 28g
- Protein: 12g

101. Awesome Baby-Face Maker

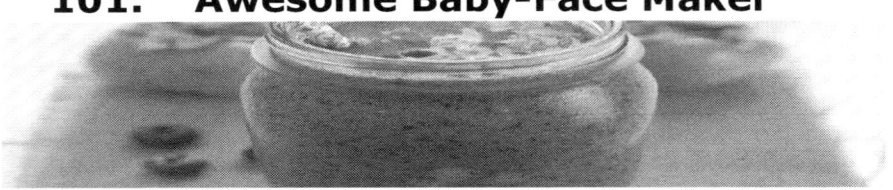

Serving: 2

Prep Time: 5 minutes

Ingredients

- 1 cup frozen blueberries
- ½ cup red bell pepper, chopped
- ½ cup seeded cucumber, diced
- 1 cup collard greens, chopped
- 3 stalks celery, chopped
- ½ teaspoon fresh ginger, peeled and minced
- ¼ cup fresh flat-leaf parsley, chopped
- 1 scoop collagen protein powder
- 1 tablespoon freshly squeezed lemon juice
- 1 tablespoon freshly squeezed lime juice
- ½ cup of water

Directions

1. Add all the ingredients except vegetables/fruits first
2. Blend until smooth
3. Add the vegetable/fruits
4. Blend until smooth
5. Add a few ice cubes and serve the smoothie

Nutrition Values

- Calories: 145
- Fat: 1g
- Carbohydrates: 28g
- Protein: 10g

102. Exotic Reishi Pear

Serving: 2

Prep Time: 5 minutes

Ingredients

- ½ cup ice
- 1 cup collard greens, chopped
- 1 pear, roughly chopped
- ¼ cup raw cashews
- 1 teaspoon reishi mushroom powder
- 1 cup unsweetened cashew milk

Directions

1. Add all the ingredients except vegetables/fruits first
2. Blend until smooth
3. Add the vegetable/fruits
4. Blend until smooth
5. Add a few ice cubes and serve the smoothie
6. Enjoy!

Nutrition Values

- Calories: 298
- Fat: 19g
- Carbohydrates: 30g
- Protein: 8g

103. The Savior of Skin

Serving: 2

Prep Time: 5 minutes

Ingredients

- ½ cup ice
- 5 large leaves romaine lettuce
- ½ cucumber, diced
- 3 celery stalks, chopped
- 1 carrot, shredded
- 1 orange, peeled and segmented
- ½ cup of water

Directions

1. Add all the ingredients except vegetables/fruits first
2. Blend until smooth
3. Add the vegetable/fruits
4. Blend until smooth
5. Add a few ice cubes and serve the smoothie

Nutrition Values

- Calories: 143
- Fat: 1g
- Carbohydrates: 30g
- Protein: 4g

104. Tangy Citrus Glass

Serving: 2

Prep Time: 5 minutes

Ingredients

- ½ cup ice
- 1 and ½ cups swiss chard, chopped
- ½ cucumber, diced
- ½ grapefruit, peeled and segmented
- ½ small apple, cored and chopped
- 1 scoop collagen protein powder
- 5 mint leaves, chopped
- 1 cup of water

Directions

1. Add all the ingredients except vegetables/fruits first
2. Blend until smooth
3. Add the vegetable/fruits
4. Blend until smooth
5. Add a few ice cubes and serve the smoothie

Nutrition Values

- Calories: 122
- Fat: 1g
- Carbohydrates: 24g
- Protein: 10g

105. Hearty Sweet Basil

Serving: 2

Prep Time: 5 minutes

Ingredients

- ½ cup ice
- 1 cup baby spinach, chopped
- ½ cucumber, diced
- ¾ cup honeydew melon cubes
- 1 handful basil leaves
- 1 and ½ teaspoons ginger, peeled and grated
- Juice of ½ lime
- 1 cup of water

Directions

1. Add all the ingredients except vegetables/fruits first
2. Blend until smooth
3. Add the vegetable/fruits
4. Blend until smooth
5. Add a few ice cubes and serve the smoothie

Nutrition Values

- Calories: 100
- Fat: 1g
- Carbohydrates: 22g
- Protein: 3g

106. The Purifier

Serving: 2

Prep Time: 5 minutes

Ingredients

- ½ cup ice
- 5 large leaves romaine lettuce
- ½ cucumber, diced
- ½ cup red bell pepper, chopped
- 1 small Granny Smith apple, cored and chopped
- 1 scoop collagen protein powder
- 5 mint leaves, chopped
- 2 tablespoons fresh-squeezed lemon juice
- 1 cup of water

Directions

1. Add all the ingredients except vegetables/fruits first
2. Blend until smooth
3. Add the vegetable/fruits
4. Blend until smooth
5. Add a few ice cubes and serve the smoothie

Nutrition Values

- Calories: 180
- Fat: 1g
- Carbohydrates: 30g
- Protein: 20g

107. Kiwi Cucumber Delight

Serving: 2

Prep Time: 5 minutes

Ingredients

- 1 cup unsweetened cashew milk
- 1 tablespoon lime juice
- 1 tablespoon chia seeds
- ½ cup cucumber, diced
- ½ small green apple, cored
- 1 kiwi, peeled
- 1 cup baby kale, chopped
- 1 cup baby spinach, chopped
- ½ cup ice

Directions

1. Add all the ingredients except vegetables/fruits first
2. Blend until smooth
3. Add the vegetable/fruits
4. Blend until smooth
5. Add a few ice cubes and serve the smoothie

Nutrition Values

- Calories: 254
- Fat: 7g
- Carbohydrates: 47g
- Protein: 8g

108. The Funky Skin Refresher

Serving: 2

Prep Time: 5 minutes

Ingredients

- ½ cup ice
- 2 cups baby spinach, chopped
- ½ cucumber, diced
- ½ cup frozen mango chunks
- ½ lime, juiced
- ½ lemon, juiced
- 1 cup of water

Directions

1. Add all the ingredients except vegetables/fruits first
2. Blend until smooth
3. Add the vegetable/fruits
4. Blend until smooth
5. Add a few ice cubes and serve the smoothie

Nutrition Values

- Calories: 103
- Fat: 1g
- Carbohydrates: 24g
- Protein: 4g

109. The Glamorous Radiance

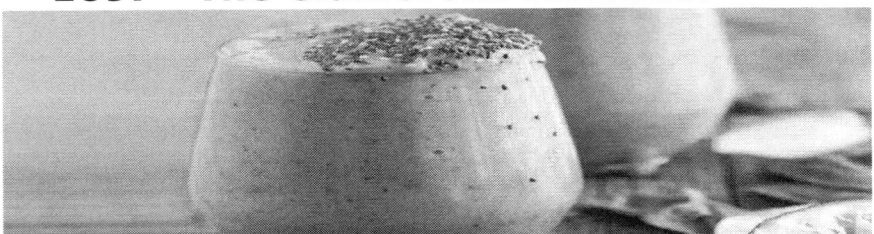

Serving: 2

Prep Time: 5 minutes

Ingredients

- ½ cup ice
- 1 cup baby spinach, chopped
- ½ cucumber, diced
- 2 kiwis, peeled
- 1/3 avocado, pit, and skin removed
- 1 scoop collagen protein powder
- 1 teaspoon freshly squeezed lime juice
- 1 cup of water

Directions

1. Add all the ingredients except vegetables/fruits first
2. Blend until smooth
3. Add the vegetable/fruits
4. Blend until smooth
5. Add a few ice cubes and serve the smoothie
6. Enjoy!

Nutrition Values

- Calories: 248
- Fat: 10g
- Carbohydrates: 29g
- Protein: 10g

Chapter 12: Kid-Friendly Smoothies
110. Delicious Creamy Choco Shake

Serving: 1

Prep Time: 10 minutes

Ingredients

- ½ cup heavy cream
- 2 tablespoons cocoa powder
- 1 pack stevia
- 1 cup of water

Directions

1. Add all the ingredients except vegetables/fruits first
2. Blend until smooth
3. Add the vegetable/fruits
4. Blend until smooth
5. Add a few ice cubes and serve the smoothie
6. Enjoy!

Nutrition Values

- Calories: 180
- Fat: 6g
- Carbohydrates: 30g
- Protein: 3g

111. Mesmerizing Strawberry and Chocolate Shake

Serving: 1

Prep Time: 10 minutes

Ingredients

- ½ cup heavy cream, liquid
- 1 tablespoon cocoa powder
- 1 pack stevia
- ½ cup strawberry, sliced
- 1 tablespoon coconut flakes, unsweetened
- 1 and ½ cups of water

Directions

1. Add all the ingredients except vegetables/fruits first
2. Blend until smooth
3. Add the vegetable/fruits
4. Blend until smooth
5. Add a few ice cubes and serve the smoothie

Nutrition Values

- Calories: 453
- Fat: 22g
- Carbohydrates: 39g
- Protein: 10g

112. The Overloaded Berry Shake

Serving: 1

Prep Time: 10 minutes

Ingredients

- ½ cup whole milk yogurt
- 1 pack stevia
- ¼ cup raspberries
- ¼ cup blackberry
- ¼ cup strawberries, chopped
- 1 tablespoon cocoa powder
- 1 tablespoon avocado oil
- 1 and ½ cups of water

Directions

1. Add all the ingredients except vegetables/fruits first
2. Blend until smooth
3. Add the vegetable/fruits
4. Blend until smooth
5. Add a few ice cubes and serve the smoothie

Nutrition Values

- Calories: 200
- Fat: 7g
- Carbohydrates: 24g
- Protein: 2g

113. The Blueberry and Chocolate Delight

Serving: 1

Prep Time: 10 minutes

Ingredients

- ½ cup whole milk yogurt
- ¼ cup blackberries
- 1 pack stevia
- 1 tablespoon MCT oil
- 1 tablespoon Dutch Processed Cocoa Powder
- 2 tablespoons Macadamia nuts, chopped
- 1 and ½ cups of water

Directions

1. Add all the ingredients except vegetables/fruits first
2. Blend until smooth
3. Add the vegetable/fruits
4. Blend until smooth
5. Add a few ice cubes and serve the smoothie

Nutrition Values

- Calories: 175
- Fat: 2g
- Carbohydrates: 33g
- Protein: 6g

114. Cool Coco-Loco Cream Shake

Serving: 1

Prep Time: 10 minutes

Ingredients

- ½ cup of coconut milk
- 2 tablespoons Dutch-processed cocoa powder, unsweetened
- 1 cup brewed coffee, chilled
- 1-2 packs stevia
- 1 tablespoon hemp seed

Directions

1. Add all the ingredients except vegetables/fruits first
2. Blend until smooth
3. Add the vegetable/fruits
4. Blend until smooth
5. Add a few ice cubes and serve the smoothie

Nutrition Values

- Calories: 337
- Fat: 11g
- Carbohydrates: 38g
- Protein: 1g

115. Healthy Chocolate Milkshake

Serving: 2

Prep Time: 10 minutes

Ingredients

- 16 ounces unsweetened almond milk, vanilla
- 1 pack stevia
- 1 Scoop Whey isolate chocolate protein powder
- ½ cup crushed ice
-

Directions

1. Add all the ingredients except vegetables/fruits first
2. Blend until smooth
3. Add the vegetable/fruits
4. Blend until smooth
5. Add a few ice cubes and serve the smoothie
6. Enjoy!

Nutrition Values

- Calories: 342
- Fat: 20g
- Carbohydrates: 43g
- Protein: 8g

116. The Cacao Super Smoothie

Serving: 1

Prep Time: 10 minutes

Ingredients

- ½ cup unsweetened almond milk, vanilla
- ½ cup half and half
- ½ avocado, peeled, pitted, sliced
- ½ cup frozen blueberries, unsweetened
- 1 tablespoon cacao powder
- 1 scoop whey vanilla protein powder
- Liquid stevia

Directions

1. Add all the ingredients except vegetables/fruits first
2. Blend until smooth
3. Add the vegetable/fruits
4. Blend until smooth
5. Add a few ice cubes and serve the smoothie
6. Enjoy!

Nutrition Values

- Calories: 300
- Fat: 13g
- Carbohydrates: 40g
- Protein: 6g

117. The Nutty Smoothie

Serving: 1

Prep Time: 10 minutes

Ingredients

- 1 tablespoon chia seeds
- 2 cups of water
- 1 ounce Macadamia Nuts
- 1-2 packets Stevia, optional
- 1-ounce Hazelnut

Directions

1. Add all the ingredients except vegetables/fruits first
2. Blend until smooth
3. Add the vegetable/fruits
4. Blend until smooth
5. Add a few ice cubes and serve the smoothie

Nutrition Values

- Calories: 170
- Fat: 5g
- Carbohydrates: 30g
- Protein: 6g

118. The Strawberry Almond Smoothie

Serving: 1

Prep Time: 10 minutes

Ingredients

- 16 ounces unsweetened almond milk, vanilla
- 1 pack stevia
- 4 ounces heavy cream
- 1 scoop vanilla whey protein
- ¼ cup frozen strawberries, unsweetened

Directions

1. Add all the ingredients except vegetables/fruits first
2. Blend until smooth
3. Add the vegetable/fruits
4. Blend until smooth
5. Add a few ice cubes and serve the smoothie

Nutrition Values

- Calories: 465
- Fat: 28g
- Carbohydrates: 57g
- Protein: 6g

119. Mixed Fruit Madness

Serving: 1

Prep Time: 10 minutes

Ingredients

- 1 cup spring mix salad blend
- 2 cups of water
- 3 medium blackberries, whole
- 1 packet Stevia, optional
- 1 tablespoon avocado oil
- 1 tablespoon coconut flakes shredded and unsweetened
- 2 tablespoons pecans, chopped
- 1 tablespoon hemp seed
- 1 tablespoon sunflower seed

Directions

1. Add all the ingredients except vegetables/fruits first
2. Blend until smooth
3. Add the vegetable/fruits
4. Blend until smooth
5. Add a few ice cubes and serve the smoothie

Nutrition Values

- Calories: 150
- Fat: 2g
- Carbohydrates: 37g
- Protein: 3g

Chapter 13: Low-Fat Smoothies
120.   The Big Blue Delight

Serving: 2

Prep Time: 5 minutes

Ingredients

- 1 tablespoon blue spirulina powder
- 1 tablespoon hemp seeds
- ¾ cup plain low-fat Greek yogurt
- 1 fresh banana
- 1 cup frozen blueberries
- 1 cup unsweetened vanilla almond milk

Directions

1. Add all the ingredients except vegetables/fruits first
2. Blend until smooth
3. Add the vegetable/fruits
4. Blend until smooth
5. Add a few ice cubes and serve the smoothie

Nutrition Values

- Calories: 245
- Fat: 6g
- Carbohydrates: 43g
- Protein: 8g

121. The Big Bomb Pop

Serving: 2

Prep Time: 5 minutes

Ingredients

- 1 tablespoon chia seeds
- ¾ cup plain low-fat Greek yogurt
- 1 cup of frozen strawberries
- 1 cup frozen blueberries
- 1 cup unsweetened vanilla almond milk

Directions

1. Add all the ingredients except vegetables/fruits first
2. Blend until smooth
3. Add the vegetable/fruits
4. Blend until smooth
5. Add a few ice cubes and serve the smoothie
6. Enjoy!

Nutrition Values

- Calories: 198
- Fat: 5g
- Carbohydrates: 30g
- Protein: 7g

122. The Pinky Swear

Serving: 2

Prep Time: 5 minutes

Ingredients

- 1 pack (3.5 ounces) frozen dragon fruit
- ¾ cup low-fat Greek yogurt
- 1 cup frozen pineapple
- 1 cup unsweetened coconut milk

Directions

1. Add all the ingredients except vegetables/fruits first
2. Blend until smooth
3. Add the vegetable/fruits
4. Blend until smooth
5. Add a few ice cubes and serve the smoothie

Nutrition Values

- Calories: 200
- Fat: 3g
- Carbohydrates: 36g
- Protein: 6g

123. A Peachy Perfect Glass

Serving: 2

Prep Time: 5 minutes

Ingredients

- 1 cup skim milk
- 1 cup frozen peaches
- 1 fresh banana
- ¾ cup Siggi's vanilla yogurt
- 1 tablespoon hemp seeds
- Dash of ground cinnamon

Directions

1. Add all the ingredients except vegetables/fruits first
2. Blend until smooth
3. Add the vegetable/fruits
4. Blend until smooth
5. Add a few ice cubes and serve the smoothie
6. Enjoy!
7.

Nutrition Values

- Calories: 208
- Fat: 6g
- Carbohydrates: 32g
- Protein: 10g

124. Slim-Jim Vanilla Latte

Serving: 2

Prep Time: 5 minutes

Ingredients

- Dash of ground cinnamon
- 1 tablespoon chia seeds
- ½ cup unsweetened vanilla almond milk
- ½ cup of leftover coffee
- 4 ice cubes
- ¾ cup Siggi's vanilla yogurt
- 2 fresh bananas

Directions

1. Add all the ingredients except vegetables/fruits first
2. Blend until smooth
3. Add the vegetable/fruits
4. Blend until smooth
5. Add a few ice cubes and serve the smoothie

Nutrition Values

- Calories: 211
- Fat: 4g
- Carbohydrates: 40g
- Protein: 7g

125. Cauliflower Cold Glass

Serving: 2

Prep Time: 5 minutes

Ingredients

- ½ cup frozen cauliflower, riced
- ½ cup of frozen strawberries
- ½ cup frozen blueberries
- ¾ cup plain low-fat Greek yogurt
- 1 fresh banana
- 1 cup unsweetened vanilla almond milk

Directions

1. Add all the ingredients except vegetables/fruits first
2. Blend until smooth
3. Add the vegetable/fruits
4. Blend until smooth
5. Add a few ice cubes and serve the smoothie

Nutrition Values

- Calories: 204
- Fat: 5g
- Carbohydrates: 33g
- Protein: 8g

126. A Batch of Slimming Berries

Serving: 2

Prep Time: 5 minutes

Ingredients

- 1 tablespoon chia seeds
- ¾ cup plain low-fat Greek yogurt
- 1 cup kale
- 1 cup of frozen mango
- 1 cup of frozen mixed berries
- 1 cup unsweetened vanilla almond milk

Directions

1. Add all the ingredients except vegetables/fruits first
2. Blend until smooth
3. Add the vegetable/fruits
4. Blend until smooth
5. Add a few ice cubes and serve the smoothie

Nutrition Values

- Calories: 200
- Fat: 5g
- Carbohydrates: 30g
- Protein: 8g

127. Fine Green Machine

Serving: 2

Prep Time: 5 minutes

Ingredients

- ¼ cup fresh avocado
- ¾ cup plain coconut yogurt
- 1 fresh banana
- 1 cup baby spinach
- 1 cup of frozen mango
- 1 cup unsweetened coconut milk

Directions

1. Add all the ingredients except vegetables/fruits first
2. Blend until smooth
3. Add the vegetable/fruits
4. Blend until smooth
5. Add a few ice cubes and serve the smoothie

Nutrition Values

- Calories: 222
- Fat: 10g
- Carbohydrates: 34g
- Protein: 6g

128. The Summer Hearty Shake

Serving: 2

Prep Time: 5 minutes

Ingredients

- 1 cup frozen blackberries
- ¾ cup Whole milk vanilla yogurt
- ½ cup unsweetened vanilla almond milk
- ½ cup of frozen strawberries
- ½ cup frozen peaches
- 1 tablespoon hemp seeds
- Dash of ground cinnamon

Directions

1. Add all the ingredients except vegetables/fruits first
2. Blend until smooth
3. Add the vegetable/fruits
4. Blend until smooth
5. Add a few ice cubes and serve the smoothie

Nutrition Values

- Calories: 187
- Fat: 6g
- Carbohydrates: 23g
- Protein: 6g

129. The Mocha Built

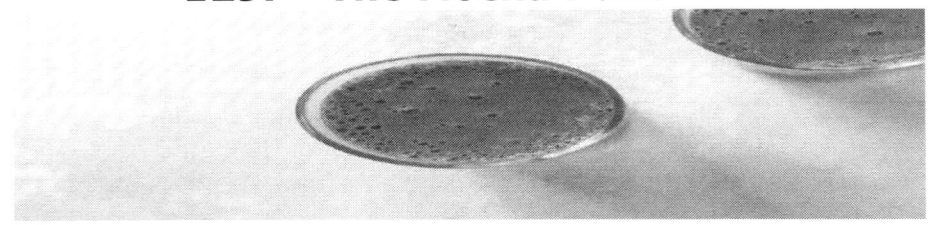

Serving: 2

Prep Time: 5 minutes

Ingredients

- 1 tablespoon cacao powder
- ½ cup of leftover coffee
- ½ cup skim milk
- ¾ cup plain low-fat Greek yogurt
- 1 cup baby spinach
- 1 cup frozen cherries
- 1 fresh banana

Directions

1. Add all the ingredients except vegetables/fruits first
2. Blend until smooth
3. Add the vegetable/fruits
4. Blend until smooth
5. Add a few ice cubes and serve the smoothie

Nutrition Values

- Calories: 178
- Fat: 3g
- Carbohydrates: 34g
- Protein: 10g

Chapter 14: Protein Smoothies

130. Sweet Protein and Cherry Shake

Serving: 2

Prep Time: 5 minutes

Ingredients

- 1 cup of water
- 3 cups spinach
- 2 bananas, sliced
- 2 cups frozen cherries
- 2 tablespoons cacao powder
- 4 tablespoons hemp seeds, shelled

Directions

1. Add all the ingredients except vegetables/fruits first
2. Blend until smooth
3. Add the vegetable/fruits
4. Blend until smooth
5. Add a few ice cubes and serve the smoothie
6. Enjoy!

Nutrition Values

- Calories: 111
- Fat: 3g
- Carbohydrates: 9g
- Protein: 13g

131. Iron And Protein Shake

Serving: 2

Prep Time: 5 minutes

Ingredients

- 2 tablespoons favorite sweetened
- 1 cup of water
- ¼ cup hemp seeds
- 2 large bananas, frozen
- 4 cups strawberries, sliced

Directions

1. Add all the ingredients except vegetables/fruits first
2. Blend until smooth
3. Add the vegetable/fruits
4. Blend until smooth
5. Add a few ice cubes and serve the smoothie

Nutrition Values

- Calories: 156
- Fat: 14g
- Carbohydrates: 1g
- Protein: 7g

132. Creamy Peachy Shake

Serving: 2

Prep Time: 5 minutes

Ingredients

- 2 scoops vanilla protein powder
- 2 cups peaches
- ¼ cup fat-free Greek yogurt
- ½ cup of orange juice

Directions

1. Add all the ingredients except vegetables/fruits first
2. Blend until smooth
3. Add the vegetable/fruits
4. Blend until smooth
5. Add a few ice cubes and serve the smoothie

Nutrition Values

- Calories: 380
- Fat: 3g
- Carbohydrates: 72g
- Protein: 20g

133. Protein-Packed Root Beer Shake

Serving: 2

Prep Time: 5 minutes

Ingredients

- ½ cup fat-free vanilla yogurt
- 1 scoop vanilla whey protein
- 1 and ½ cups root beet
- 1 scoop vanilla casein protein

Directions

1. Add all the ingredients except vegetables/fruits first
2. Blend until smooth
3. Add the vegetable/fruits
4. Blend until smooth
5. Add a few ice cubes and serve the smoothie

Nutrition Values

- Calories: 677
- Fat: 56g
- Carbohydrates: 39g
- Protein: 16g

134. Almond And Choco-Brownie Shake

Serving: 2

Prep Time: 5 minutes

Ingredients

- ½ chocolate brownie bar, chopped
- ¼ cup almonds, chopped
- 1 scoop chocolate whey protein
- 1 cup fat-free milk

Directions

1. Add all the ingredients except vegetables/fruits first
2. Blend until smooth
3. Add the vegetable/fruits
4. Blend until smooth
5. Add a few ice cubes and serve the smoothie

Nutrition Values

- Calories: 578
- Fat: 35g
- Carbohydrates: 69g
- Protein: 17g

135. Raspberry And White Chocolate Shake

Serving: 2

Prep Time: 5 minutes

Ingredients

- 2 scoops whey vanilla protein powder
- 1 tablespoon chia seeds
- 1 tablespoon white chocolate chips
- 2 tablespoons water
- 1 cup coconut milk, unsweetened
- ¾ cup frozen raspberries

Directions

1. Add all the ingredients except vegetables/fruits first
2. Blend until smooth
3. Add the vegetable/fruits
4. Blend until smooth
5. Add a few ice cubes and serve the smoothie

Nutrition Values

- Calories: 574
- Fat: 35g
- Carbohydrates: 34g
- Protein: 34g

136. Peppermint And Dark Chocolate Shake Delight

Serving: 2

Prep Time: 5 minutes

Ingredients

- ¼ teaspoon peppermint extract
- 1 scoop chocolate whey protein powder
- 2 tablespoons cocoa powder
- Pinch of salt
- 1 cup almond milk
- 1 large frozen banana
- 2-3 large ice cubes

Directions

1. Add all the ingredients except vegetables/fruits first
2. Blend until smooth
3. Add the vegetable/fruits
4. Blend until smooth
5. Add a few ice cubes and serve the smoothie

Nutrition Values

- Calories: 374
- Fat: 26g
- Carbohydrates: 26g
- Protein: 16g

137. Spiced Up Banana Shake

Serving: 2

Prep Time: 5 minutes

Ingredients

- 2 scoops vanilla protein powder
- ½ teaspoon ground cinnamon
- 1/8 teaspoon ground nutmeg
- 2 ripe bananas
- 12 ice cubes

Directions

1. Add all the ingredients except vegetables/fruits first
2. Blend until smooth
3. Add the vegetable/fruits
4. Blend until smooth
5. Add a few ice cubes and serve the smoothie

Nutrition Values

- Calories: 506
- Fat: 30g
- Carbohydrates: 56g
- Protein: 12g

138. Mad Mocha Glass

Serving: 2

Prep Time: 5 minutes

Ingredients

- 4 ice cubes
- 1 scoop 100% chocolate whey protein
- ½ scoop vanilla protein powder
- 6 ounces of water
- 6 ounces cold coffee

Directions

1. Add all the ingredients except vegetables/fruits first
2. Blend until smooth
3. Add the vegetable/fruits
4. Blend until smooth
5. Add a few ice cubes and serve the smoothie

Nutrition Values

- Calories: 306
- Fat: 4g
- Carbohydrates: 43g
- Protein: 28g

139. Lemon And Cranberry Shake

Serving: 2

Prep Time: 5 minutes

Ingredients

- 4 ice cubes
- 1 and ½ cups of vanilla frozen yogurt
- 1-2 scoops 100% vanilla whey protein powder
- 2 cups mixed berries
- ½ teaspoon lemon zest
- 12 ounces cranberry juice
- 1 tablespoon lemon juice

Directions

1. Add all the ingredients except vegetables/fruits first
2. Blend until smooth
3. Add the vegetable/fruits
4. Blend until smooth
5. Add a few ice cubes and serve the smoothie

Nutrition Values

- Calories: 172
- Fat: 5g
- Carbohydrates: 35g
- Protein: 13g

Chapter 15: Weight-Loss Smoothies
140. Hearty Dandelion Smoothie

Serving: 2

Prep Time: 5 minutes

Ingredients

- 1 cup crushed ice
- 1 tablespoon spirulina
- 1 orange
- ¾ avocado, cubed
- 2 bananas, diced
- 1 cup dandelion leaves, chopped

Directions

1. Add all the ingredients except vegetables/fruits first
2. Blend until smooth
3. Add the vegetable/fruits
4. Blend until smooth
5. Add a few ice cubes and serve the smoothie

Nutrition Values

- Calories: 166
- Fat: 3g
- Carbohydrates: 35g
- Protein: 5g

141. Apple And Zucchini Medley

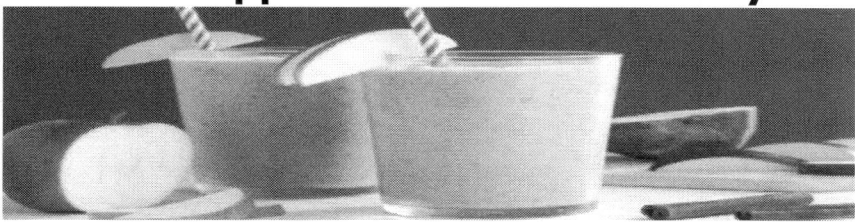

Serving: 2

Prep Time: 5 minutes

Ingredients

- 1 cup crushed ice
- 1 jalapeno pepper
- 2 stalk celeries, diced
- ¾ avocado, cubed
- 2 apples, quartered

Directions

1. Add all the ingredients except vegetables/fruits first
2. Blend until smooth
3. Add the vegetable/fruits
4. Blend until smooth
5. Add a few ice cubes and serve the smoothie

Nutrition Values

- Calories: 282
- Fat: 2g
- Carbohydrates: 62g
- Protein: 4g

142. Flax And Kiwi Spinach Smoothie

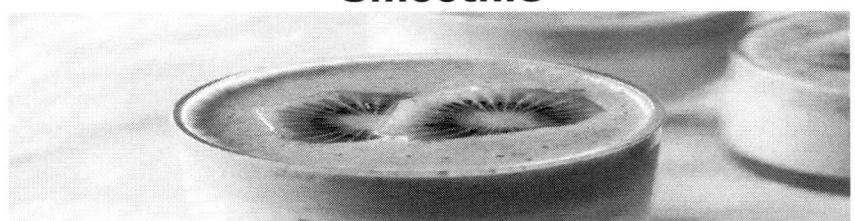

Serving: 2

Prep Time: 5 minutes

Ingredients

- 1 cup crushed ice
- 3 tablespoons ground flax
- 3 kiwis, diced
- 1 stalk celery, chopped
- 1 banana, chopped
- 2 apples, quartered
- 1 cup spinach, chopped

Directions

1. Add all the ingredients except vegetables/fruits first
2. Blend until smooth
3. Add the vegetable/fruits
4. Blend until smooth
5. Add a few ice cubes and serve the smoothie

Nutrition Values

- Calories: 142
- Fat: 7g
- Carbohydrates: 16g
- Protein: 6g

143. Cucumber Kale and Lime Apple Smoothie

Serving: 2

Prep Time: 5 minutes

Ingredients

- 1 cup crushed ice
- 1 cucumber, diced
- ¼ cup raspberries, chopped
- 1 lime, juiced
- 1 avocado, diced
- 2 apples, quartered
- 1 cup kale, chopped

Directions

1. Add all the ingredients except vegetables/fruits first
2. Blend until smooth
3. Add the vegetable/fruits
4. Blend until smooth
5. Add a few ice cubes and serve the smoothie

Nutrition Values

- Calories: 291
- Fat: 2g
- Carbohydrates: 38g
- Protein: 7g

144. Banana And Spinach Raspberry Smoothie

Serving: 2

Prep Time: 5 minutes

Ingredients

- 1 tablespoons cilantro
- 1 cup crushed ice
- 1 tablespoon ground flax seeds
- ½ cup raspberries
- 2 dates
- 2 bananas
- 1 cup spinach, chopped

Directions

1. Add all the ingredients except vegetables/fruits first
2. Blend until smooth
3. Add the vegetable/fruits
4. Blend until smooth
5. Add a few ice cubes and serve the smoothie

Nutrition Values

- Calories: 120
- Fat: 2g
- Carbohydrates: 30g
- Protein: 3g

145. Flax And Almond Butter Smoothie

Serving: 2

Prep Time: 5 minutes

Ingredients

- 1 teaspoon flax seed
- ½ cup crushed ice
- 3 strawberries
- 1 banana, frozen
- 2 cups spinach
- 2 tablespoons almond butter
- ½ cup plain yogurt

Directions

1. Add all the ingredients except vegetables/fruits first
2. Blend until smooth
3. Add the vegetable/fruits
4. Blend until smooth
5. Add a few ice cubes and serve the smoothie

Nutrition Values

- Calories: 147
- Fat: 7g
- Carbohydrates: 21g
- Protein: 4g

146. Leeks And Broccoli Cucumber Glass

Serving: 2

Prep Time: 5 minutes

Ingredients

- 1 cup crushed ice
- 1 tablespoon Matcha
- ½ cup leaf lettuce, chopped
- ½ cup lettuce, chopped
- 1 lime, juiced
- 2 cucumbers, diced
- 2 leeks, chopped
- 2 tablespoons cashew butter
- 1 cup broccoli, diced

Directions

1. Add all the ingredients except vegetables/fruits first
2. Blend until smooth
3. Add the vegetable/fruits
4. Blend until smooth
5. Add a few ice cubes and serve the smoothie

Nutrition Values

- Calories: 219
- Fat: 6g
- Carbohydrates: 6g
- Protein: 4g

147. Straight Up Avocado and Kale Smoothie

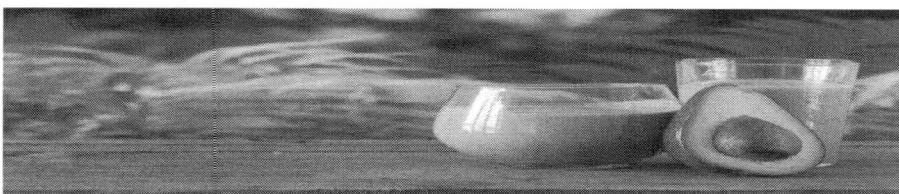

Serving: 2

Prep Time: 5 minutes

Ingredients

- 1 tablespoon spirulina
- 1 cup chamomile tea
- 1 tablespoon Chia seeds
- 1 celery stalk
- 1 cup cucumber
- ½ avocado, diced
- 1 cup kale, chopped

Directions

1. Add all the ingredients except vegetables/fruits first
2. Blend until smooth
3. Add the vegetable/fruits
4. Blend until smooth
5. Add a few ice cubes and serve the smoothie

Nutrition Values

- Calories: 236
- Fat: 6g
- Carbohydrates: 46g
- Protein: 4g

148. Apple Broccoli Smoothie

Serving: 2

Prep Time: 5 minutes

Ingredients

- 1 tablespoon seaweed, crushed
- 1 cup ice, crushed
- 1 celery stalk, diced
- 1 tablespoon cilantro, chopped
- 1 cup broccoli, diced
- 1 apple, quartered

Directions

1. Add all the ingredients except vegetables/fruits first
2. Blend until smooth
3. Add the vegetable/fruits
4. Blend until smooth
5. Add a few ice cubes and serve the smoothie

Nutrition Values

- Calories: 223
- Fat: 1g
- Carbohydrates: 51g
- Protein: 9g

149. Zucchini Apple Smoothie

Serving: 2

Prep Time: 5 minutes

Ingredients

- 1 and ½ cups crushed ice
- 1 tablespoon Spirulina
- 1 lemon, juiced
- 1 stalk celery
- ¾ avocado
- 2 apples, quartered
- ½ cup zucchini, diced

Directions

1. Add all the ingredients except vegetables/fruits first
2. Blend until smooth
3. Add the vegetable/fruits
4. Blend until smooth
5. Add a few ice cubes and serve the smoothie

Nutrition Values

- Calories: 80
- Fat: 4g
- Carbohydrates: 11g
- Protein: 2g

Chapter 16: Alkaline Smoothies
150. Strawberry And Clementine Mix

Serving: 2

Prep Time: 5 minutes

Ingredients

- 8 ounces strawberries, fresh
- 1 banana, chopped into chunks
- 2 Clementine's/ Mandarins

Directions

1. Peel the clementine's and remove seeds
2. Add the listed ingredients to your blender/food processor and blend until smooth
3. Serve chilled and enjoy!

Nutrition Values

- Calories: 590
- Fat: 57g
- Carbohydrates: 17g
- Protein: 12g

151. Strawberry And Watermelon Smoothie

Serving: 2

Prep Time: 5 minutes

Ingredients

- 1 cup coconut milk yogurt
- ½ cup strawberries
- 2 cups fresh watermelon
- 1 banana, diced

Directions

1. Add the listed ingredients to your blender/food processor and blend until smooth
2. Serve chilled and enjoy!

Nutrition Values

- Calories: 160
- Fat: 5g
- Carbohydrates: 33g
- Protein: 1.8g

152. Watermelon Berry Smoothie

Serving: 2

Prep Time: 5 minutes

Ingredients

- 2 cups watermelon
- 1 and ½ cups berries, mixed
- ¼ cup fresh mint leaves
- 2 fresh lemon leaves
- 2 fresh lemons, juiced
- 1 cup evamor

Directions

1. Add the listed ingredients to your blender/food processor and blend until smooth
2. Serve chilled and enjoy!

Nutrition Values

- Calories: 122
- Fat: 1g
- Carbohydrates: 26g
- Protein: 2.4g

153. Cucumber And Spinach Glass

Serving: 2

Prep Time: 5 minutes

Ingredients

- ½ cucumber, sliced
- 1/3 cup spinach, chopped
- ½ green apple, diced
- ¾ cup of water

Directions

1. Add the listed ingredients to your blender/food processor and blend until smooth
2. Serve chilled and enjoy!

Nutrition Values

- Calories: 86
- Fat: 0.5g
- Carbohydrates: 21g
- Protein: 2g

154. Broccoli Green Smoothie

Serving: 2

Prep Time: 5 minutes

Ingredients

- ½ cup broccoli
- 1 cup spinach, chopped
- 1 banana, diced
- 1 apple, diced
- 1 lemon, peeled
- 1 carrot, peeled and chopped

Directions

1. Add the listed ingredients to your blender/food processor and blend until smooth
2. Serve chilled and enjoy!

Nutrition Values

- Calories: 71
- Fat: 0.3g
- Carbohydrates: 18g
- Protein: 1.3g

155. A Sweet Green Mix

Serving: 2

Prep Time: 5 minutes

Ingredients

- 1 cup pomegranate juice
- 1 mango, diced
- ½ cup wheatgrass
- 2 tablespoons flax seeds

Directions

1. Add the listed ingredients to your blender/food processor and blend until smooth
2. Serve chilled and enjoy!

Nutrition Values

- Calories: 379
- Fat: 5g
- Carbohydrates: 80g
- Protein: 6g

156. Almond And Spinach Glass

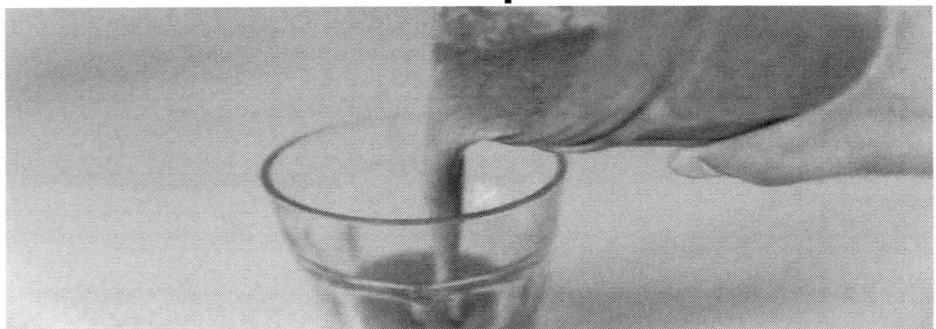

Serving: 2

Prep Time: 5 minutes

Ingredients

- 2 cups fresh spinach, chopped
- 1 and ½ cups of almond milk
- ½ cup of coconut water
- 3 cups fresh pineapple, cubed
- 2 tablespoons unsweetened coconut flakes

Directions

1. Add the listed ingredients to your blender/food processor and blend until smooth
2. Serve chilled and enjoy!

Nutrition Values

- Calories: 200
- Fat: 4g
- Carbohydrates: 40g
- Protein: 3.6g

157. Pear And Kale Glass

Serving: 2

Prep Time: 5 minutes

Ingredients

- 1 ripe pear, cored and chopped
- 2 cups kale, chopped
- ¼ cup mint leaves
- 1 cup of water
- 1 cup apple juice

Directions

1. Add the listed ingredients to your blender/food processor and blend until smooth
2. Serve chilled and enjoy!

Nutrition Values

- Calories: 135
- Fat: 0.3g
- Carbohydrates: 32g
- Protein: 3g

158. Peach And Banana Glass

Serving: 2

Prep Time: 5 minutes

Ingredients

- 1 ripe peach, chopped
- 1 banana, diced
- 1 and ¼ ounces spinach
- 1 teaspoon agave syrup
- 1 cup of coconut water

Directions

1. Add the listed ingredients to your blender/food processor and blend until smooth
2. Serve chilled and enjoy!

Nutrition Values

- Calories: 120
- Fat: 0.7g
- Carbohydrates: 28g
- Protein: 2g

159. Almond And Carrot Smoothie

Serving: 2

Prep Time: 5 minutes

Ingredients

- 1 cup unsweetened almond milk
- 1 tablespoon almond butter
- 1 scoop protein powder
- ½ banana
- 1 teaspoon cinnamon, ground
- 3 carrots, shredded

Directions

1. Add the listed ingredients to your blender/food processor and blend until smooth
2. Serve chilled and enjoy!

Nutrition Values

- Calories: 400
- Fat: 14g
- Carbohydrates: 42g
- Protein: 28g

160. Protein Spinach Shake

Serving: 2

Prep Time: 5 minutes

Ingredients

- 2 cups spinach
- ½ banana, diced
- 1 tablespoon protein powder
- ½ teaspoon cinnamon
- ½ cup yogurt
- 1 and ½ cups unsweetened almond milk

Directions

1. Add the listed ingredients to your blender/food processor and blend until smooth
2. Serve chilled and enjoy!

Nutrition Values

- Calories: 396
- Fat: 21g
- Carbohydrates: 40g
- Protein: 20g

161. Basil Strawberry Delight

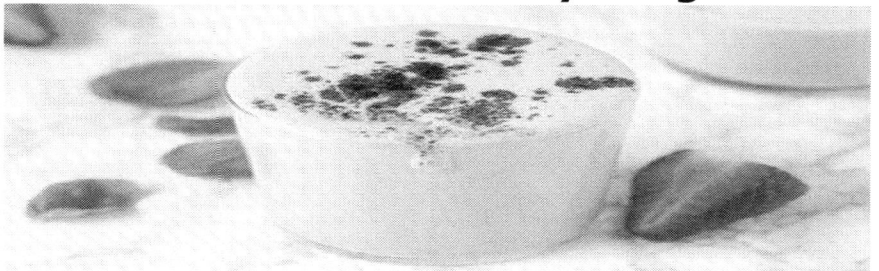

Serving: 2

Prep Time: 5 minutes

Ingredients

- 1 cup kale
- ½ banana, diced
- 3 strawberries
- ¼ cup basil, chopped
- 1 tablespoon flax seeds
- 1 and ½ cups unsweetened coconut milk

Directions

1. Add the listed ingredients to your blender/food processor and blend until smooth
2. Serve chilled and enjoy!

Nutrition Values

- Calories: 203
- Fat: 9g
- Carbohydrates: 28g
- Protein: 6g

162. Cabbage And Chia Delight

Serving: 2

Prep Time: 5 minutes

Ingredients

- 1/3 cup cabbage
- 1 cup cold unsweetened coconut milk
- 1 tablespoon chia seeds
- ½ cup cherries
- ½ cup spinach

Directions

1. Add coconut milk to your blender
2. Cut cabbage and add to your blender
3. Place chia seeds in a coffee grinder and chop to powder; brush the powder into a blender
4. Pit the cherries and add them to the blender
5. Wash and dry the spinach and chop
6. Add to the mix
7. Cover and blend on low followed by medium
8. Taste the texture and serve chilled!

Nutrition Values

- Calories: 155
- Fat: 3g
- Carbohydrates: 33g
- Protein: 2g

163. Grapefruit Spinach Smoothie

Serving: 2

Prep Time: 5 minutes

Ingredients

- 2 grapefruits, peeled and deseeded
- 1 avocado, diced
- 2 cups baby spinach, chopped
- 4 ounces of water
- 10 drops liquid stevia

Directions

1. Add the listed ingredients to your blender/food processor and blend until smooth
2. Serve chilled and enjoy!

Nutrition Values

- Calories: 253
- Fat: 20g
- Carbohydrates: 20g
- Protein: 4g

164. Plain Coconut Smoothie

Serving: 2

Prep Time: 5 minutes

Ingredients

- 4 ounces fresh coconut meat
- 1 cup of coconut water
- 1 tablespoon coconut oil
- 1 banana, diced

Directions

1. Add the listed ingredients to your blender/food processor and blend until smooth
2. Serve chilled and enjoy!

Nutrition Values

- Calories: 669
- Fat: 52g
- Carbohydrates: 53g
- Protein: 7g

165. Lovely Detox Smoothie

Serving: 2

Prep Time: 5 minutes

Ingredients

- 1 cup of coconut water
- 1 avocado, diced
- 1 cucumber, diced
- 1 cup spinach, chopped
- 1 tablespoon ginger, chopped
- 1 tablespoon coconut butter

Directions

1. Add the listed ingredients to your blender/food processor and blend until smooth
2. Serve chilled and enjoy!

Nutrition Values

- Calories: 310
- Fat: 22g
- Carbohydrates: 22g
- Protein: 5g

166. Blueberry Avocado Smoothie

Serving: 2

Prep Time: 5 minutes

Ingredients

- ½ cup blueberries
- 1 avocado
- ½ cup unsweetened coconut milk
- 1 teaspoon chia seeds

Directions

1. Add the listed ingredients to your blender/food processor and blend until smooth
2. Serve chilled and enjoy!

Nutrition Values

- Calories: 389
- Fat: 34g
- Carbohydrates: 20g
- Protein: 5g

167. Lemon And Pineapple Smoothie

Serving: 2

Prep Time: 5 minutes

Ingredients

- 2 cups pineapple
- ½ lemon, peeled
- 1 teaspoon turmeric
- 1 cup almond milk

Directions

1. Add the listed ingredients to your blender/food processor and blend until smooth
2. Serve chilled and enjoy!

Nutrition Values

- Calories: 362
- Fat: 23g
- Carbohydrates: 30g
- Protein: 4g

168. Raspberry Chia Seeds

Serving: 2

Prep Time: 5 minutes

Ingredients

- 2 cups spinach
- 1 cup of coconut milk
- 1 cup of coconut water
- 3 cups raspberries
- 1 tablespoon chia seeds
- 1 teaspoon vanilla extract

Directions

1. Add the listed ingredients to your blender/food processor and blend until smooth
2. Serve chilled and enjoy!

Nutrition Values

- Calories: 425
- Fat: 31g
- Carbohydrates: 35g
- Protein: 8g

169. Avocado And Orange Glass

Serving: 2

Prep Time: 5 minutes

Ingredients

- 1 and ½ cup of orange juice
- ½ cup of water
- ¼ cup avocado, diced
- ½ teaspoon lime zest, grated
- 2 cups mango, diced

Directions

1. Add the listed ingredients to your blender/food processor and blend until smooth
2. Serve chilled and enjoy!

Nutrition Values

- Calories: 220
- Fat: 5g
- Carbohydrates: 45g
- Protein: 3g

170. Apricot And Spinach Smoothie

Serving: 2

Prep Time: 5 minutes

Ingredients

- 2 cups spinach
- 1 apricot
- 1 cup of coconut water
- ½ tablespoon coconut oil

Directions

1. Add the listed ingredients to your blender/food processor and blend until smooth
2. Serve chilled and enjoy!

Nutrition Values

- Calories: 135
- Fat: 8g
- Carbohydrates: 15g
- Protein: 4g

171. Cantaloupe Lemon Smoothie

Serving: 2

Prep Time: 5 minutes

Ingredients

- 1 cup cantaloupe, cubed
- 1 teaspoon fresh lemon juice
- ¼ cup of coconut milk
- 10 drops liquid stevia
- 1 tablespoon fresh mint, chopped

Directions

1. Add the listed ingredients to your blender/food processor and blend until smooth
2. Serve chilled and enjoy!

Nutrition Values

- Calories: 195
- Fat: 14g
- Carbohydrates: 16g
- Protein: 3g

172. Frosty Watermelon Smoothie

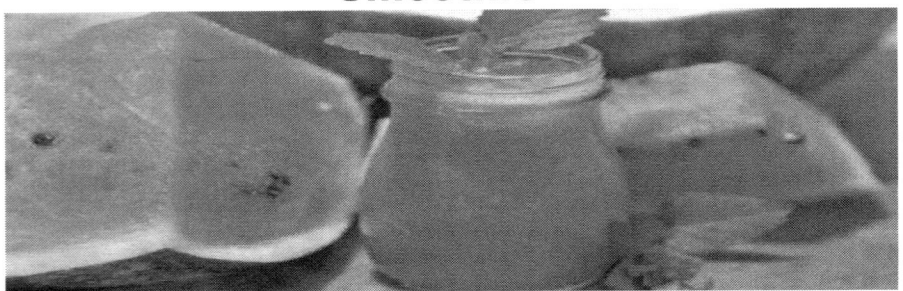

Serving: 2

Prep Time: 5 minutes

Ingredients

- ¾ cup of coconut water
- 2 cups watermelon, cut into chunks
- ½ banana
- 2 tablespoon fresh lime juice
- 1 teaspoon maple syrup

Directions

1. Add the listed ingredients to your blender/food processor and blend until smooth
2. Serve chilled and enjoy!

Nutrition Values

- Calories: 217
- Fat: 1g
- Carbohydrates: 54g
- Protein: 5g

173. Lush Cherry Mix

Serving: 2

Prep Time: 5 minutes

Ingredients

- ½ cup ripe cherries
- Juice of 1 lemon
- 1 cup of coconut milk
- 1 avocado, cubed
- ¼ cup spinach
- Few slices of cucumber, peeled

Toppings

- Handful of pistachios
- Handful of raisins
- 1 slice lemon

Directions

1. Blend all the ingredients until smooth
2. Add a few ice cubes to make it chilled
3. Add your desired toppings

Nutrition Values

- Calories: 375
- Fat: 14g
- Carbohydrates: 65g
- Protein: 4g

174. Crafty Cucumber Smoothie

Serving: 2

Prep Time: 5 minutes

Ingredients

- Handful of ice
- Handful of spinach
- 1 kiwi fruit, cubed
- ½ banana, diced
- ¼ cucumber
- ¼ cup of coconut milk

Directions

1. Add the listed ingredients to your blender/food processor and blend until smooth
2. Serve chilled and enjoy!

Nutrition Values

- Calories: 112
- Fat: 2g
- Carbohydrates: 27g
- Protein: 2g

175. Balanced Alkaline Veggie Cubes

Serving: 2

Prep Time: 5 minutes

Ingredients

- Alkaline water as needed
- ½ cup parsley leaves, chopped
- 3 cups packed collard green leaves, chopped
- 3 cups packed kale, chopped
- 1 large cucumber, peeled and cut
- ¾ cup fresh lime, squeezed

Directions

1. Add the listed ingredients to your blender/food processor and blend until smooth
2. Serve chilled and enjoy!

Nutrition Values

- Calories: 20
- Fat: 0.2g
- Carbohydrates: 5g
- Protein: 11g

176. Blueberry And Banana Smoothie

Serving: 2

Prep Time: 5 minutes

Ingredients

- ½ cup of water
- ½ cup of soy milk
- ½ cup ice
- ½ tablespoon hemp seeds, optional
- ½ tablespoon ground flaxseed
- 1 teaspoon alkaline green powder
- ½ cup blueberries
- 1 ripe banana, diced

Directions

1. Add the listed ingredients to your blender/food processor and blend until smooth
2. Serve chilled and enjoy!

Nutrition Values

- Calories: 251
- Fat: 6g
- Carbohydrates: 44g
- Protein: 10g

177. Pineapple Green Smoothie

Serving: 2

Prep Time: 5 minutes

Ingredients

- ½ lemon, squeezed
- 1 tablespoon fresh ginger, chopped
- 2 cups frozen pineapple, diced
- 4 cups spinach
- 2 cups water, filtered

Directions

1. Add the listed ingredients to your blender/food processor and blend until smooth
2. Serve chilled and enjoy!

Nutrition Values

- Calories: 172
- Fat: 1g
- Carbohydrates: 35g
- Protein: 9g

178. Tri-Berry Smoothie

Serving: 2

Prep Time: 5 minutes

Ingredients

- 2 Medjool dates, halved and pitted
- ½ cup quinoa, cooked
- ½ cup frozen blackberries
- ½ cup frozen raspberries
- 1 cup frozen blueberries
- 1 cup alkaline water

Directions

1. Add the listed ingredients to your blender/food processor and blend until smooth
2. Serve chilled and enjoy!

Nutrition Values

- Calories: 222
- Fat: 2g
- Carbohydrates: 46g
- Protein: 8g

179. Alkaline Lime Smoothie

Serving: 2

Prep Time: 5 minutes

Ingredients

- 1 and ½ cups ice
- Pinch of salt
- 20 drops liquid stevia
- 2 limes, peeled and halved
- 2 tablespoons lime zest, grated
- ½ medium cucumber, chopped
- 1 medium avocado, pitted and peeled
- 2 cups baby spinach
- ½ cup of coconut meat
- ¾ cup of coconut water

Directions

1. Add the listed ingredients to your blender/food processor and blend until smooth
2. Serve chilled and enjoy!

Nutrition Values

- Calories: 84
- Fat: 1g
- Carbohydrates: 18g
- Protein: 3g

180. The Antioxidant Booster

Serving: 2

Prep Time: 5 minutes

Ingredients

- Alkaline water as needed
- ½ lemon, juiced
- ½ garlic, chopped
- 1 cucumber, diced
- 1 avocado, cubed
- Handful of lettuce
- 1 tomato, diced
- 2 broccoli heads, diced
- Handful of spinach
- Handful of kale

Directions

1. Add the listed ingredients to your blender/food processor and blend until smooth
2. Serve chilled and enjoy!

Nutrition Values

- Calories: 253
- Fat: 4g
- Carbohydrates: 40g
- Protein: 18g

181. Raw Green Smoothie

Serving: 2

Prep Time: 5 minutes

Ingredients

- 2 tablespoons omega-rich oil
- 1 teaspoon salt
- ½ head romaine lettuce, chopped
- ¼ medium onion, chopped
- 1 lime, peeled and chopped
- ¼ bunch cilantro
- 1 avocado
- ½ English cucumber, peeled and chopped
- 1 tomato, chopped

Directions

1. Add the listed ingredients to your blender/food processor and blend until smooth
2. Serve chilled and enjoy!

Nutrition Values

- Calories: 298
- Fat: 26g
- Carbohydrates: 20g
- Protein: 4g

182. The Green Goddess

Serving: 2

Prep Time: 5 minutes

Ingredients

- 1 cup of water
- ½ lemon, peeled and chopped
- ½ cup frozen pineapple chunks
- 1 cup frozen mango chunks
- 1 medium carrot, chopped
- ½ teaspoon chia seeds
- ¼ teaspoon turmeric
- ¼ teaspoon ground cinnamon
- ½ tablespoon ground ginger
- ½ celery stalk, chopped
- 1 apple, peeled and chopped
- ¼ cup kale
- 2 cups baby spinach

Directions

1. Add the listed ingredients to your blender/food processor and blend until smooth
2. Serve chilled and enjoy!

Nutrition Values

- Calories: 225
- Fat: 1g
- Carbohydrates: 56g
- Protein: 3g

183. Morning Alkaline Blend

Serving: 2

Prep Time: 5 minutes

Ingredients

- 1 cup spinach
- 3 apples, cored and cubed
- 2 celery stalks, diced
- 3 cucumbers, chopped
- 2 large carrots, diced

Directions

1. Add the listed ingredients to your blender/food processor and blend until smooth
2. Serve chilled and enjoy!

Nutrition Values

- Calories: 247
- Fat: 10g
- Carbohydrates: 38g
- Protein: 4g

184. Original Sleepy Bug

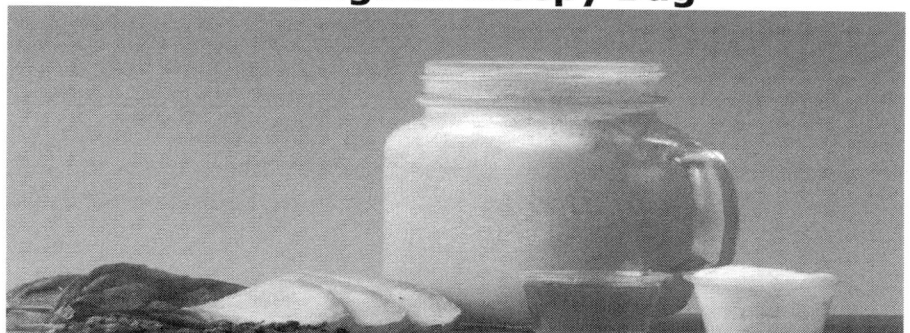

Serving: 2

Prep Time: 5 minutes

Ingredients

- 1 cup fennel tea infusion
- 1 cup almond milk
- 1 cup watermelon, chopped
- 1 green apple
- ½ cup pomegranate
- ½ inch ginger
- Stevia to sweeten

Directions

1. Add the listed ingredients to your blender
2. Blend until smooth
3. Add a bit of stevia if you want more sweetness
4. Serve chilled and enjoy!

Nutrition Values

- Calories: 156
- Fat: 11g
- Carbohydrates: 14g
- Protein: 4g

185. Coconut And Mango Meal

Serving: 2

Prep Time: 5 minutes

Ingredients

- 1 teaspoon spirulina
- 1 cup of frozen mango
- 1 cup unsweetened coconut milk
- ½ cup spinach

Directions

1. Cut mangoes and dice them
2. Add mango, a cup of unsweetened coconut milk, a teaspoon of Spirulina, and spinach to the blender
3. Blend on low to medium until smooth
4. Check the texture and serve chilled!

Nutrition Values

- Calories: 234
- Fat: 3g
- Carbohydrates: 53g
- Protein: 5g

186. Tangy Lettuce Detox

Serving: 2

Prep Time: 5 minutes

Ingredients

- 8 ounces strawberries, fresh
- 1 banana, chopped into chunks
- 2 Clementine's/ Mandarins

Directions

1. Add the listed ingredients to your blender/food processor and blend until smooth
2. Serve chilled and enjoy!

Nutrition Values

- Calories: 140
- Fat: 1.3g
- Carbohydrates: 31g
- Protein: 31g

187. Tri-Berry Banana Smoothie

Serving: 2

Prep Time: 5 minutes

Ingredients

- 2 tablespoons agave
- 1 cup spring water
- ½ cup blueberries
- 1 burro banana, peeled
- ½ cup raspberries
- ½ cup strawberries

Directions

1. Add the listed ingredients to your blender/food processor and blend until smooth
2. Serve chilled and enjoy!

Nutrition Values

- Calories: 130
- Fat: 5g
- Carbohydrates: 26g
- Protein: 5g

188. Nut Packed Papaya Meal

Serving: 2

Prep Time: 5 minutes

Ingredients

- 1 papaya, deseeded
- 3 dates, pitted
- 1 burro banana, peeled
- ¼ key lime, juiced
- 1 cup spring water

Directions

1. Add the listed ingredients to your blender/food processor and blend until smooth
2. Serve chilled and enjoy!

Nutrition Values

- Calories: 152
- Fat: 4g
- Carbohydrates: 33g
- Protein: 2.4g

189. Dandelion Greens

Serving: 2

Prep Time: 5 minutes

Ingredients

- ½ burro banana, peeled
- ½ apple, cored and deseeded
- ½ cucumber, deseeded
- ½ cup dandelion greens

Directions

1. Add the listed ingredients to your blender/food processor and blend until smooth
2. Serve chilled and enjoy!

Nutrition Values

- Calories: 317
- Fat: 11g
- Carbohydrates: 42g
- Protein: 10g

190. Cucumber And Tamarind Meal

Serving: 2

Prep Time: 5 minutes

Ingredients

- 1 cup herb tea
- ½ tablespoon tamarind pulp
- ½ cucumber, deseeded
- 1-ounce arugula
- ½ key lime, juiced
- ¼ teaspoon salt
- 1/8 teaspoon cayenne pepper

Directions

1. Add the listed ingredients to your blender/food processor and blend until smooth
2. Serve chilled and enjoy!

Nutrition Values

- Calories: 110
- Fat: 0.5g
- Carbohydrates: 30g
- Protein: 2g

191. Clean Cantaloupe Smoothie

Serving: 2

Prep Time: 5 minutes

Ingredients

- ½ cantaloupe, peeled, deseeded, sliced
- ¼ cup herb tea
- ½ burro banana, peeled
- ½ cup soft-jelly coconut water

Directions

1. Add the listed ingredients to your blender/food processor and blend until smooth
2. Serve chilled and enjoy!

Nutrition Values

- Calories: 114
- Fat: 0.6g
- Carbohydrates: 27g
- Protein: 1.8g

192. Refreshing Watermelon Breather

Serving: 2

Prep Time: 5 minutes

Ingredients

- ½ key lime, juiced and zest
- ½ watermelon, peeled, deseeded, and cubed

Directions

1. Add the listed ingredients to your blender/food processor and blend until smooth
2. Serve chilled and enjoy!

Nutrition Values

- Calories: 55
- Fat: 1.3g
- Carbohydrates: 9g
- Protein: 0.9g

193. Watercress Detox Delight

Serving: 2

Prep Time: 5 minutes

Ingredients

- 1 key lime, juiced
- ½ Avocado, peeled and pitted
- ½ cup watercress

Directions

1. Add the listed ingredients to your blender/food processor and blend until smooth
2. Serve chilled and enjoy!

Nutrition Values

- Calories: 150
- Fat: 10g
- Carbohydrates: 8g
- Protein: 7g

194. Figs Smoothie

Serving: 2

Prep Time: 5 minutes

Ingredients

- 1 cup spring water
- 2 strawberries
- ½ cup figs
- ½ burro banana, peeled

Directions

1. Peel the clementine's and remove seeds
2. Add the listed ingredients to your blender/food processor and blend until smooth
3. Serve chilled and enjoy!

Nutrition Values

- Calories: 234
- Fat: 2g
- Carbohydrates: 53g
- Protein: 7g

195. Hearty Green Glass

Serving: 2

Prep Time: 5 minutes

Ingredients

- 1 avocado
- 1 handful spinach, chopped
- Cucumber, 2-inch slices, peeled
- 1 lime, chopped
- A handful of grapes, chopped
- 5 dates, stoned and chopped
- 1 cup apple juice (fresh)

Directions

1. Add all the listed ingredients to your blender
2. Blend until smooth
3. Add a few ice cubes and serve the Smoothie
4. Enjoy!

Nutrition Values

- Calories: 177
- Fat: 7g
- Carbohydrates: 29g
- Protein: 4g

196. Classic Banana and Ginger Mix

Serving: 2

Prep Time: 5 minutes

Ingredients

- 1 banana, sliced
- ¾ cup vanilla yogurt
- 1 tablespoon honey
- ½ teaspoon ginger, grated

Directions

1. Add the listed ingredients to your blender and blend until smooth
2. Serve chilled!

Nutrition Values

- Calories: 128
- Fat: 2g
- Carbohydrates: 25g
- Protein: 4g

197. The Ginger and Kale Ale

Serving: 2

Prep Time: 5 minutes

Ingredients

- Handful of kale
- Handful of spinach
- 2 broccoli heads
- 1 tomato
- Handful of lettuce
- 1 avocado, cubed
- 1 cucumber, cubed
- Juice of ½ lemon
- Pineapple juice as needed

Directions

1. Add all the listed ingredients to your blender
2. Blend until smooth
3. Add a few ice cubes and serve the Smoothie

Nutrition Values

- Calories: 140
- Fat: 0g
- Carbohydrates: 18g
- Protein: 1g

198. Anti-Oxidizing Glass

Serving: 2

Prep Time: 5 minutes

Ingredients

- 1 whole ripe avocado
- 4 cups organic baby spinach leaves
- 1 cup of filtered water
- Juice of 1 lemon
- 1 English cucumber, chopped
- 3 stems fresh parsley
- 5 stems fresh mint
- 1-inch piece of fresh ginger
- 2 large ice cubes

Directions

1. Add all the listed ingredients to your blender
2. Blend until smooth
3. Add a few ice cubes and serve the Smoothie

Nutrition Values

- Calories: 200
- Fat: 15g
- Carbohydrates: 16g
- Protein: 3g

199. Fresh Orange Smoothie

Serving: 2

Prep Time: 5 minutes

Ingredients

- 1 orange, peeled
- ¼ cup fat-free yogurt
- 2 tablespoons frozen orange juice concentrate
- ¼ teaspoon vanilla extract
- 4 ice cubes

Directions

1. Add the listed ingredients to your blender and blend until smooth
2. Serve chilled!

Nutrition Values

- Calories: 173
- Fat: 1g
- Carbohydrates: 38g
- Protein: 4g

200. Tart Cherry and Greens Smoothie

Serving: 1

Prep Time: 10 minutes

Cook Time: 0 minute

Ingredients

- 1 cup tart cherry, frozen and pitted
- 1/2 cup kale, stems removed and chopped
- 1/2 cup broccoli florets
- 1/2 cup orange juice, squeezed
- 1/2 cup cold water

How To

1. Add puree cherries, kale, orange juice, broccoli to your blender
2. Blend it until smooth and creamy
3. Add remaining ingredients and blend it until you get a smooth mixture
4. Serve and enjoy!

Nutrition Values

- Calories: 157
- Fat: 0.6g
- Carbohydrates: 37g
- Protein: 4g

201. Beans, Peaches and Greens Smoothie

Serving: 1

Prep Time: 10 minutes

Cook Time: 0 minute

Ingredients

- 1 cup peaches, frozen
- 1/4 can white beans
- 1/2 cup almond milk
- 1/4 cup almond
- 1/4 cup quick-cooking oats
- 1/8 teaspoon cinnamon
- Pinch of nutmeg
- 1 cup packed lettuce
- 1/4 cup Italian parsley
- 6 ice cubes

Directions:

1. Add all ingredients to your blender
2. Blend it until you get a smooth and creamy mixture
3. Serve chilled and enjoy!

Nutrition Values
- Calories: 346
- Fat: 11g
- Carbohydrates: 55g
- Protein: 12g

Printed in Great Britain
by Amazon